First published in 2006 by
Essence Quisine
Redhouse Interchange
Adwick-Le-Street
Doncaster
South Yorkshire

Cover Shot: The entrance to the walled garden

Pages 2-3: The walled kitchen garden during September

Pages 4-5: A week in the life of Patrick at work in the kitchen

ISBN 10    0-9554607-0-0

ISBN 13    978-0-9554607-0-8


Typeset in California FB
Printed by Butler and Tanner Limited. United Kingdom

# Contents

# About the Author and the Book

Patrick Thompson, 31, has worked as a chef since he was 15 years old. He has always had a real passion for sourcing quality ingredients, producing fantastic food and enjoying all styles of cuisine. As the youngest winner, to date, of the Roux Scholarship competition in 1998, Patrick has enjoyed a full and varied career taking him to a 3 Michelin Star restaurant in Paris, and as far as the Caribbean.

Since 2002 Patrick has been employed as the personal chef to The Lord Kirkham CVO and family. Working in both Yorkshire and France, Patrick's cooking philosophy and menu planning are invariably based around produce from the 3 acre walled kitchen garden in Yorkshire, and the bustling markets of the French Riviera.

With the help of this book you can enjoy preparing over 100 seasonal recipes that should encourage you to make the most of the produce from your own kitchen garden or greenhouse. If you do not have a kitchen garden or greenhouse then hopefully, you will be inspired to seek out the freshest local and seasonal ingredients to test your culinary skills.

Whether you are preparing a simple lunch, or entertaining guests for a special dinner, you will surely find something that appeals here.

# Foreword

I don't know much about cooking in general, or recipes in particular. But I do know quite a lot about eating fine food, and about Chef Patrick Thompson.

Indeed I wager that I have eaten more meals cooked by Patrick than anyone else, and a greater variety, too - whether they were prepared to be eaten with a knife and fork, just a fork, spoon, chopsticks or fingers. I also know the simple equation that never fails to produce the best meal:

1 Great Chef + highest quality ingredients = SUPERB FOOD

Patrick Thompson IS a Great Chef: classically trained, with international experience, yet still just 31 years of age, so that all his expertise is combined with the open-minded enthusiasm and energy of youth.

Through this beautiful book, you and I are able to share some of Patrick's immense knowledge and passion for good food and fine cooking.

It is a book that is special in many ways. Because it was produced without commercial or financial strictures, and because of the remarkable input Patrick has made of both commitment and imagination.

More than that, though, it can make a special difference to you. Patrick to use a colloquialism is 'the business'. And with his help, through this outstanding book, you could be 'the business' in the kitchen, too.

Congratulations, Chef - and good cooking and eating to all of you.

The Lord Kirkham CVO

# Introduction

We are amidst changing times when it comes to food and eating. On one hand, we are being encouraged to meticulously study what we consume and to eat healthier, fresher and more locally produced food. On the other, we are bombarded with marketing and advertisements in many forms, and the lure of fast food that is easily available.

Over recent years the government and various food groups as well as large sections of the media have been telling us – the public – to pay attention to where we buy our food from, as well as its nutritional content, our calorie intake and our exercise levels. This, I applaud, and I implore you to take steps, however large or small, to make the most of the fresh, seasonal and healthy produce available to us all.

Everybody requires food – it is the fuel for life and therefore food is a necessity. There is no doubt that food is and should be appealing; this is what makes us so tempted by products offered through media and retail advertising. I believe, along with many others, that food is there to be enjoyed but at the same time it must provide us with all the nutrition that we need to live.

I urge everybody to take more time to understand the origin and life cycle of the food they eat and respect the natural ingredients a little more. Many will argue that the time restraints of modern living prevents them from growing and cooking their own food but given the importance of eating we can all do a little better, whether it is by growing some small simple salads and herbs or by shopping for fresh, natural foods and then taking a little time to prepare a simple dish.

Cooking doesn't have to be a chore. For sure, you will find recipes in this book that require more effort than everyday cooking, but then you will also find some tasty dishes that are easily achievable.

My recipes reflect contemporary cooking and eating rather than traditional preparations and dishes. These traditional recipes are just as good though when prepared using fresh, seasonal food.

Nowadays, with the buying power of our supermarkets, we can buy most fruits and vegetables all year round. Whilst this may be attractive to the customer I think it is important not to overlook our own traditional seasonal produce here in Britain. Obviously, nobody wants to eat pea's everyday in the summer or leeks everyday during the winter, but a little understanding and respect of the seasons goes a long way.

Provenance [*the place of origin of something*] is of great importance to me and I encourage you to search out the best locally produced foods in season; develop good relationships with the suppliers; understand more about what you are eating; try to achieve a more balanced diet and if at all possible, start to grow some fruit, vegetables and herbs, or make full use of the food you already grow.

Happy cooking and Bon Appétit.

*Patrick J Thompson*

# A note about Organic produce

Over the last 10 years there has been a meteoric increase in interest and awareness surrounding organic produce. I have a particular desire to use organic meat, poultry and dairy produce as organically rearing and feeding animals is more ethical and I believe that this results in a better product. As for fruit and vegetables, I am blessed with the produce from Lord Kirkham's kitchen garden which is organically biased. The kitchen gardeners only use chemicals as a tonic to boost an otherwise flagging fruit tree or vegetable and such a treatment is rare. My key stipulation concerning the purchasing of fresh fruit and vegetables is that the time between the product being picked or harvested, and time it arrives on the plate is kept to an absolute minimum.

I have included the following information about the organic movement which is also available on the Soil Association website; www.soilassociation.org

*The Soil Association is the UK's leading environmental charity promoting sustainable, organic farming and championing human health.*

*Here are some of organic farming's main features:*

- *Organic farming severely restricts the use of artificial chemical fertiliser and pesticides.*
- *Instead, organic farmers rely on developing a healthy, fertile soil and growing a mixture of crops.*
- *Animals are reared without the routine use of drugs, antibiotics and wormers common in intensive livestock farming.*

*Why are more people choosing organic?*

- *Food Safety: Organic farmers, as far as possible, avoid using unnecessary chemical sprays. Food additives linked to asthma and heart diseases are among those banned under organic standards.*
- *The environment: Organic farming is friendlier to the environment so there is a much greater diversity of birds, butterflies and insects on organic farms. Organic standards ban the use of GM technology.*
- *Animal welfare: Organic farming requires animals to be kept in more natural, free-range conditions with a more natural diet.*
- *Taste: Many people tell us they buy organic food because they believe it tastes better.*

# A note about food miles:

As well as the increase in demand for organic produce, there has also been a lot of scrutiny cast upon the distance that our food can travel between field and plate. Whilst I am not recommending you stop eating produce from Asia, New Zealand and the USA for example, I would echo sentiments that we should all look closer to home for our food, before we encourage the long distance transportation of goods that increase pollution through the fuel used. As well as the threat to our environment we must consider the negative impact on those who work in the food industry in under-developed countries. Always look for 'Fairtrade' produce when purchasing food that originates in these countries.

# A guide to weight and volume conversions

I have shown my recipe quantities in both Metric and Imperial measurements. However, I have listed a conversion chart below to assist when weighing and measuring ingredients if you are altering the number of people you are cooking for.

## Weight conversions (approximate)

| Metric Weight | Imperial Weight |
|---|---|
| 15g | ½ oz |
| 25g | 1oz |
| 50g | 2oz |
| 75g | 2 ½oz |
| 100g | 3 ½oz |
| 125g | 4oz |
| 150g | 5oz |
| 175g | 6oz |
| 200g | 7oz |
| 225g | 8oz |
| 250g | 9oz |
| 300g | 10oz |
| 350g | 12oz |
| 400g | 13oz |
| 450g | 16oz (1lb) |
| 500g | 17oz |
| 900g | 2lb |
| 1kg | 2lb 2oz |

## Volume (approximate)

| Metric | Imperial |
|---|---|
| 25ml | 1 fl oz |
| 50ml | 2 fl oz |
| 100ml | 3 ½ fl oz |
| 125ml | 4 fl oz |
| 150ml | 5 fl oz |
| 200ml | 7 fl oz |
| 250ml | 9 fl oz |
| 275ml | 10 fl oz ( ½ pint) |
| 300ml | 11 fl oz |
| 350ml | 12 fl oz |
| 500ml | 18 fl oz |
| 1lt | 1 ¾ pints |
| 2lt | 2 ½ pints |

# A guide to cooking temperatures

There are vast selections of ovens available to the consumer nowadays. I have listed an approximate conversion guide below. However, if in any doubt, it is best to use an oven thermometer to ensure you are cooking at the correct temperature. I always use a fan assisted oven; if you have a conventional oven then you may need to extend the cooking times slightly.

| °C | °F | Gas Mark |
|---|---|---|
| 70 | 150 | ¼ |
| 80 | 175 | ¼ |
| 100 | 200 | ½ |
| 110 | 225 | ½ |
| 130 | 250 | 1 |
| 140 | 275 | 1 |
| 150 | 300 | 2 |
| 170 | 325 | 3 |
| 180 | 350 | 4 |
| 190 | 375 | 5 |
| 200 | 400 | 6 |
| 220 | 425 | 7 |
| 230 | 450 | 8 |
| 240 | 475 | 8 |
| 250 | 500 | 9 |
| 275 | 525 | 9 |
| 290 | 550 | 9 |

# A guide to cooking equipment

The best advice I can give you here is to use or buy the highest quality cookware you can. The following list represents the equipment I have used in the preparation of recipes throughout this book.

## Larger pieces of equipment:

Electric mixer with paddle, dough hooks and balloon whisk
Electric ice cream machine
Electric table top deep fat fryer
Electric food blender/liquidiser
Electric hand held stick blender
A set of accurate kitchen scales
Sturdy chopping boards
Pasta/noodle making machine
Large heavy based saucepan for stock making (approx 6lts/ 7 ½ pints capacity)
Selection of heavy based saucepans
Large non-stick frying pans
Smaller non-stick frying pans
Cast iron frying pans
Griddle pan
Crepe pan
Copper sugar pan
Wok

## Smaller pieces of equipment:

Set of good quality sharp kitchen knives
Good quality sharpening steel or stone
Kitchen scissors
Fish scaler
Fish tweezers for removing small bones
Potato peeler, apple corer, garlic press and olive stoner
Wooden spoons, slotted metal spoon, metal spider spoon, ladle, fish slice, tongs, spatula
Selection of sieves and colanders of varying mesh size
Pastry brush, piping bags and nozzles, non-stick baking mats and silicon paper
Fluted and plain cutters, rolling pin, hand whisk
Plain round stainless steel rings of varying size
Flan rings and cases of varying size
Grater and nutmeg grater
Baking trays of varying depth and size
Cooling trays
Terrine/pate moulds of varying size
Round bottomed stainless steel mixing bowls
Selection of ramekins and Dariole moulds in varying size
Mandolin cutter
Sugar thermometer
A set of good quality food storage containers
Selection of measuring jugs in varying size

# A guide to the recipes

Each recipe in the book has been given a 'chef's hat' rating to indicate the degree of difficulty.

Signifies a basic recipe achievable with the minimum of fuss.

Signifies a recipe that requires a little more thought and planning,
and a moderate understanding of culinary techniques.

Signifies a recipe that is complex and consists of several components.
These recipes are ideal for entertaining and for the more ambitious cook.

# A guide to help you make the most of The Essence

Measurements and quantities.

All of the recipes contained in this book are listed in both metric and imperial units. A table on page 12 will assist with any conversions that you may need to make.

Throughout the recipes you will find the following abbreviations:

| | | |
|---|---|---|
| Tsp | = | a level teaspoonful |
| Tbsp | = | a level tablespoonful |
| lt | = | litre |
| fl oz | = | fluid ounce |
| kg | = | kilogram |
| g | = | gram |
| oz | = | ounce |
| mm | = | millimetre |
| cm | = | centimetre |

All eggs are large unless otherwise stated.

A note on using your own cooking equipment.

I have specified on page 14 which pieces of cooking equipment you may need in order to prepare the dishes in The Essence. Obviously, there are many different types and brands of oven, blender, mixing machine and other electrical gadgets. I would recommend that if you are in any doubt as to cooking times, temperatures or the correct operation of the appliance, you refer to the manufacturer's guidelines.

Cooking with gas or electricity.

Cooking with gas or electricity can vary cooking times, with factors such as gas pressure and the different wattages of your appliances altering cooking times slightly. The timescales given in the book for baking, roasting, boiling and the like can differ if your home's gas pressure is low or your electric oven is particularly hot. I recommend you take these factors into account when following recipes.

Cooking terms

As you read through the recipes, you will no doubt find several cookery terms with which you are unfamiliar. On pages 281 and 282 I have listed a comprehensive glossary to assist you in fully understanding each recipe. I have also highlighted these cooking terms in italic typeset where they first appear in each recipe.

A note about eggs

Some recipes in The Essence require the use of raw or lightly cooked egg. Whilst I suggest you only use organic or free-range eggs, I recommend anybody who is in a high-risk health group or who is pregnant to avoid these recipes.

# A guide to menu planning and composition

I advise that, as with any task you may be attempting, I advise that when planning a meal, whether it be an informal lunch or special dinner party, you give proper thought to planning, preparation and execution in order to achieve the best results. The following tips may help you:

- Identify what it is you are aiming to achieve in your menu from the outset.
- Pay particular attention to the seasonality of produce and whether or not it is readily available. The recipes in The Essence are divided into the four seasons; so this will assist you in compiling a suitably seasonal menu.
- Don't work beyond your own or your kitchen's capabilities. It is much better to keep the menu simple for the first few dinner parties you host, and then challenge yourself once your confidence has increased.
- Plan and take into account the range of colours, tastes, textures, aromas and nutritional balance within your menu. Aim for a varied menu that encompasses all of these things. For example, when it comes to different sauces within a menu, I like to serve vinaigrettes, light cream or delicately spiced dressings to begin the meal, then follow these with a richer and more robustly flavoured sauce, and finally finish with a sweet, spiced or fruity style sauce.
- Read recipes carefully; allow ample time for preparation and practice if unsure. I suggest that you weigh, measure and prepare all the ingredients you will need for a recipe before you start cooking.
- Remember, an organised and efficient cook is a successful one.
- Clean as you go. No clean, no go.

A series of seasonal menus are suggested on pages 273 – 279, along with wine recommendations to complement your cuisine. For an informal lunch I would serve a maximum of three courses. In the evening however, I love to showcase a variety of produce through four, five or even six smaller dishes. This style of menu would include one or two 'taster' courses such as an intensely flavoured soup served in an espresso cup or a jelly presented in a shot glass or an elegant egg cup.

When you present the food to your guests it can be visually enhanced by the use of individual crockery. When I plan a menu I always imagine on what kind and style of plate or bowl the food would look best. You may be surprised by the difference the right serving crockery can make.

# The Kitchen Garden produce

I am fortunate enough to have access to a wealth of different fruits, vegetables and herbs in the kitchen garden on Lord Kirkham's estate. Here I have listed the varieties of produce that I used in the preparation of recipes for this book, but you may, of course, have your own favourite variety of fruit or vegetable. I trust that reading the list and appreciating the diversity of ingredients available will encourage you to investigate the origin of your shopping basket, and hopefully grow some of your own fresh produce.

| | |
|---|---|
| Apples: | Ashmeads Kernal, Golden Noble, Blenheim Orange, Egremont Russet, Cox's Pomona, George Neal, Ellison's Orange, Ribston Pippin, Sunset |
| Apricots: | Moorpark |
| Beetroot: | Chioggia Pink, Boltardy, Burpees Golden, Cylindra |
| Broad beans: | The Sutton, Scarlet Flowered, Imperial Green Long Pod, Aquadulce Claudia |
| Brussels sprouts: | Bedford, Fillbasket, Falstaff |
| Cabbage: | January King, Red Drumhead, Ormskirk, April, Primo, Greyhound, Christmas Drumhead, Tundra |
| Carrots: | Chantenay Red Cored, Parmex, Yellowstone, Purple Haze, Ingot, Healthmaster, January King |
| Cauliflower: | White Excel, Romanesco, Mayflower |
| Celeriac: | Monarch |
| Celery: | Victoria |
| Cherries: | Sunburst, Stella, Morello |
| Courgettes: | Parador, Green Bush, Tricolour, Rondi Di Nizza |
| Cucumbers: | Kyoto, Burpless Tasty Green |
| Dwarf Beans: | Nomad, Golddukat, Purple Teepee, The Prince, The Tunner |
| Fennel: | Montebianco, Goal, Cantino |
| Figs: | Brown Turkey, White Marseille |
| French beans: | Helda, Empress, Neckar Queen |
| Garlic: | Long Keeper, Mediterranean |
| Gooseberries: | Pax, Invicta, Careless |
| Leeks: | Neptune, Musselburgh, Titan |
| Lettuces: | Sonette, Valdor, Tom Thumb, Fristina, Lollo Rossa, Little Gem, Iceberg, Rusty, Raddichio |
| Kale: | Noro, Red Boar, Black Tuscany |
| Mangetout: | Sugar Pea Norli, Carouby de Maussane |

| | |
|---|---|
| Medlar: | Nottingham |
| Onions: | Rijnsbuger, Giant Ailsa Craig, Red Baron |
| Pak choi: | Canton Dwarf, Hanakan |
| Parsnips: | Tender and True, Avonresister |
| Peaches: | Rochester, Duke of York, Peregrine, Barrington |
| Pears: | Catallic, Conference, Doyenne du Comice, Onward, Beth, Merton Pride |
| Peas: | Oregon Sugar Pod, Sancho, Sugar Snap, Early Onward, Alderman |
| Potatoes: | Anya, Red Duke of York, Foremost, Adora, Charlotte, Royal Kidney, Ratte, Pink Fir Apple, Blue Salad, Arran Pilot, Desiree |
| Plums: | Victoria, Opal, Cambridge Gage, Early Laxton, Oullions Golden Gage |
| Pumpkins: | Mars, Wee B Little |
| Quince: | Vranja |
| Radish: | French Breakfast, Black Spanish Round |
| Raspberries: | Glen Moy, Glen Prosen, Fallgold, Autumn Bliss, Leo |
| Redcurrants: | Redlake, Jonkheer van Tets, White Versailles (whitecurrants) |
| Rhubarb: | Champagne, Stockbridge Arrow, Victoria |
| Rocket: | Sky Rocket, Rucola |
| Shallots: | Red Sun, Topper, Golden Gourmet, Atlantic |
| Spinach: | Perpetual, Bordeaux |
| Spring onions: | White Lisbon, Furio |
| Sprouting broccoli: | Nine Star Perennial, Purple Sprouting Early and Late |
| Squash: | Avalon, Nutty Delicia, Hasta la Pasta, Butternut Sprinter |
| Strawberries: | Elsanta, Aromel, Migonette |
| Swiss chard: | Rainbow Chard Bright Lights |
| Tomatoes: | Golden Sunrise, Tigerello, Red Alert, Roma, Alicante, Shirley, Gardener's Delight |
| Turnips: | Snowball, Golden Ball |

# Spring

Officially, spring begins towards the end of April but the kitchen gardener is governed by the season's weather, temperature and location. Once the risk of frost has dissipated then the sowing season can begin in earnest. Some varieties of potato, onion and the like will already have gone into the ground but this is the time when salads and many vegetables can be planted out. The keen gardener may have access to a heated greenhouse where fruit and vegetables can be 'brought on' or 'forced' earlier than otherwise may be the case outside. If you are new to growing your own produce then you may need a little patience whilst waiting for the correct time to sow and reap the rewards.

I have based this spring section on the months of April, May and June and on the availability from our own walled garden where we are fortunate to have access to greenhouses, heated glasshouses and cold frames, as well as rich organically biased cultivated soil outside.

Obviously, the recipes are applicable for whenever your own produce is ready or whenever you find the new season's produce on your local market or farm. You will find recipes for asparagus, broad beans, globe artichokes, lettuce, young beetroots, strawberries, rhubarb and gooseberries amongst others.

# New season garden vegetables and herbs with Old Cotswold Legbar egg and Jabugo ham

This is a plate of fantastic fresh and unique food. The choices of vegetables and herbs are entirely up to you and dependant on what is available. The eggs used here are from an old classic breed and are pastel in colour and have a thicker, harder shell than their hybrid counterparts. The hens have more stamina and stronger muscles as they range over a wide area of grassland, enjoying a natural cereal based diet that gives the yolk a deep rich yellow glow. Jabugo is a village in the Sierra de Arácnea (Spain), which provides the ideal climate to produce this famous ham. The Iberian pig leg is cured for between 18 and 30 months and has a wonderful, soft texture with a flavour in a class of its own.

Serves 6

300g/ 10oz Romanesco cauliflower florets
300g/ 10oz purple sprouting broccoli florets
30 small spears of asparagus
1 head spring cabbage
100g/ 3 ½ oz sea kale stems
12 radishes
Handful of mixed picked herbs, rinsed
6 Old Cotswold Legbar eggs
6 tbsp olive oil
6 very thin slices Jabugo ham
Extra virgin olive oil to serve.
Sea salt & black pepper

*Chefs tip*
*Blanching vegetables in boiling water,*
*and then refreshing them in iced water*
*retains their colour and crispness, as well*
*helping to preserve their nutritional content.*

1. Trim, rinse and *blanch* the cauliflower, broccoli, asparagus and sea kale separately in boiling salted water until *al dente*. *Refresh* in iced water, drain and reserve.
2. Break the spring cabbage into small pieces and steam for 20 seconds. Refresh in iced water, drain and reserve.
3. Wash, trim and thinly slice the radishes.
4. Heat the olive oil in a non-stick frying pan (moderate heat) and gently fry the eggs. Season and keep warm by covering the pan in tin foil.
5. On six serving plates, place an egg in the centre and arrange the vegetables around the egg. Sprinkle with the herbs and place a slice of the Jabugo on top of the egg.
6. Drizzle with extra virgin olive oil, season and serve.

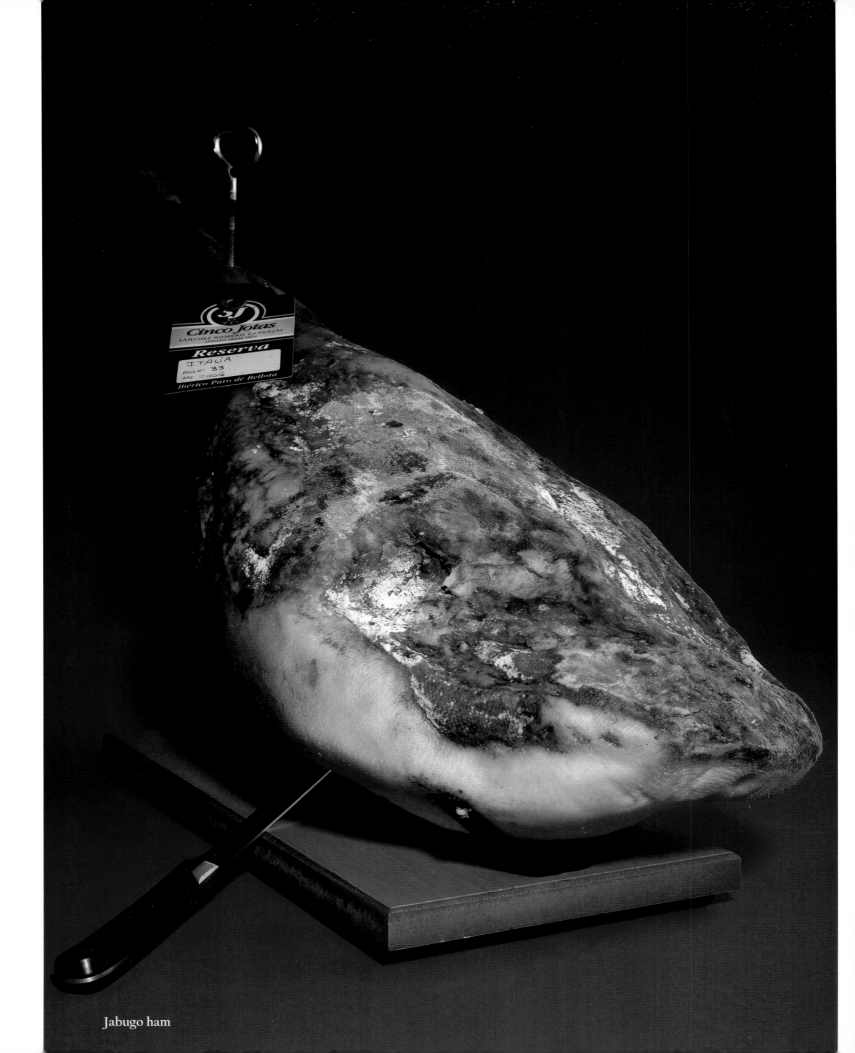

Jabugo ham

Old Cotswold Legbar Eggs

# Asparagus salad with lemon zest, fresh almonds and Pecorino cheese

With its delicate flavour, new season asparagus does not need to be overpowered by a multitude of ingredients. Here, I have simply added lemon and Pecorino cheese to enhance the flavour, and toasted almonds for texture. You could of course cook the asparagus on the griddle instead of blanching it as I have done here.
Serves 6

60 stalks of tender asparagus, about 10cm/ 4" in length
1 large organic lemon
18 fresh almonds or 75g/ 2 ½ oz flaked almonds
200g/ 7oz rocket (washed)
75g/ 2 ½ oz piece of Pecorino cheese
100ml/ 3 ½ fl oz extra virgin olive oil
25ml/ 1 fl oz white balsamic vinegar
Sea salt & black pepper

*Chefs tip*
*I only use asparagus during the short*
*British season, which runs from late April*
*to late June. White asparagus is also available*
*and would work equally well here.*

1. Trim the asparagus by removing a little of the base and peeling if the outer skin is particularly thick. Wash well. *Blanch* the asparagus in a pan of boiling salted water for 1 minute or until *al dente*. *Refresh* in iced water, pat dry on kitchen paper. Reserve.
2. Peel the lemon and cut the *zest* into very fine *julienne*. Place in a pan of cold water, bring to the boil, strain and refresh. Reserve.
3. Shell the fresh almonds, and toast under a hot grill until golden, or just toast the flaked almonds.
4. Using a potato peeler, make shavings from the Pecorino cheese.
5. Whisk the vinegar and lemon juice together and gradually whisk in the olive oil. Season to taste.
6. In a large bowl, combine the asparagus and rocket. Drizzle over the olive oil dressing and gently toss together. Divide equally onto serving plates. Sprinkle the asparagus with the almonds, lemon zest and cheese shavings. Finish with a touch of sea salt and a turn of black pepper and drizzle over any remaining dressing.

# Printanière of asparagus and broad beans with aioli

Printanière [a dish of spring vegetables] aptly describes this colourful, tasty starter. I have used aioli, a sauce similar to mayonnaise, to thicken and further flavour the cooking liquor.
Serves 6

For the principal ingredients:
36 stems of tender asparagus
450g/ 1lb podded broad beans
125g/ 4oz washed baby spinach leaves
2 tbsp coarsely chopped flat parsley

For the aioli/mayonnaise:
150ml/ 5 fl oz white wine vinegar
4 black peppercorns
½ bay leaf
2 free-range organic egg yolks
3 garlic cloves, peeled & finely crushed
250ml/ 9 fl oz groundnut oil
Juice of ½ lemon
Sea salt & black pepper

To prepare the aioli/mayonnaise:
1. *Reduce* the vinegar together with the peppercorns and bay leaf by half in a saucepan over a medium heat. Strain through a sieve and cool.
2. Whisk the egg yolks and garlic with the vinegar for a few minutes until pale.
3. Slowly trickle in the oil, whisking constantly until the oil has completely *emulsified*. Season to taste with the salt and lemon juice.

For the principal ingredients:
1. Wash, trim and peel the asparagus if the outer skin is particularly thick. Cut in half. *Blanch* the stalks and tips separately in boiling salted water until just tender. Reserving the cooking juice, remove and drain the asparagus. Keep warm by covering in Clingfilm.
2. Repeat the blanching process with the broad beans. Shell the beans and keep warm.
3. Working quickly (the vegetables are cooked and ready to go), take 350ml/ 12 fl oz of the cooking liquor from the asparagus, add the crushed garlic and reduce by half in a clean pan.
4. Turn the heat setting to low and gradually whisk in the mayonnaise taking care not to boil it. Once the mayonnaise has been incorporated, add the chopped parsley. Keep warm.
5. Using shallow serving bowls divide and arrange the asparagus, broad beans and spinach leaves. Spoon over the sauce and sprinkle with a touch of sea salt. Serve.

# Simple broad bean soup with a poached free-range egg

This is a simple soup to prepare, and one that captures the taste of broad beans perfectly.
Serves 6

450g/ 1lb podded broad beans
50ml/ 2 fl oz olive oil
1 medium finely chopped onion
1 garlic clove, peeled & crushed
1 lt/ 1 ¾ pints vegetable stock (see basics)
Sea salt & black pepper
100ml/ 3 ½ fl oz crème fraîche
6 free-range organic eggs
100ml/ 3 ½ fl oz white wine vinegar
Olive oil
Chopped chives

1. In a large saucepan, heat the olive oil and then add the onion. *Sweat* over a medium heat until softened.
2. Add the broad beans and sweat for 2-3 minutes. Add the vegetable stock, bring to the boil and then simmer for 10 minutes. Transfer to a blender and blend until very smooth.
3. Season to taste and whisk in the crème fraîche. Reserve.
4. To *poach* the eggs: boil 2lts/ 3 ½ pints of water with the vinegar and reduce the heat to a simmer. Whisk the water in a circular fashion to create a whirlpool effect. Crack one egg into the centre of the whirlpool and poach until the white has just set. Remove the egg to a warmed plate, cover with Clingfilm and then repeat to poach all the eggs. You could use two pans to save time.
5. Reheat the soup and transfer the eggs to six warmed soup bowls.
6. Pour the soup around the eggs and garnish with chopped chives and a drizzle of olive oil.

# Sauté of organic free-range chicken
# with a light asparagus sauce

As you can see from the photograph, this is a very attractive dish to look at, but actually very simple to prepare. Home-grown asparagus and a locally sourced free-range chicken will give you an opportunity to explain the dish to your guests with pride and satisfaction at the quality produce on offer.
Serves 6

6 small (approx 100g/ 3 ½ oz each) organic free-range skinless chicken breasts
2 tbsp organic plain flour
50ml/ 2 fl oz olive oil
½ garlic clove, peeled & crushed
18 stems tender asparagus
4 spring onions (washed & thinly sliced)
150ml/ 5 fl oz dry white wine
150ml/ 5 fl oz vegetable stock (see basics)
150ml/ 5 fl oz double cream or crème fraîche
30g/ 1 oz chilled, diced, unsalted butter
Sea salt & black pepper

*Chefs tip*
*To crush garlic cloves, simply roughly chop the cloves on a board and sprinkle with a little coarse sea salt. Take a strong, wide bladed knife and crush the garlic by pressing the blade against the board in a semi-circular motion.*

Trim the asparagus, remove and discard any woody base and peel if the outer skin is particularly thick. Wash well. Cut the asparagus in half.
*Blanch* the asparagus in boiling salted water for 1 minute or until *al dente*. *Refresh* in iced water, drain, pat dry. Reserve the asparagus tips for the garnish and use the bottom half for the sauce.
To make the sauce, heat a quarter of the olive oil in a small saucepan and *sweat* the bottom halves for 30 seconds. Add the vegetable stock and *reduce* by a quarter. Then add the double cream and reduce by a further quarter. Transfer to a blender and blend until very smooth. Season to taste and cool.
Remove any excess sinew or visible fat from the chicken breasts and cut each breast into six equal sized pieces. Season the flour and then lightly dust the chicken in the flour.
Heat the remaining olive oil in a large frying pan and *sauté* the chicken pieces over a medium heat until lightly golden and cooked through (approximately 10 minutes). Keep warm.
Remove the chicken from the pan and drain off any excess fat. Add the white wine to the pan and reduce this by half over a high heat.
Add the smooth asparagus sauce, bring almost to the boil and then slowly whisk the chilled butter in until completely *emulsified*. Cool to approximately 80°C/ 175°F.
Transfer the sauce to a tall sided saucepan or measuring jug and whisk with an electric hand blender until frothy. (The addition of an ice cube can help to make a light frothy sauce)
Arrange the chicken and asparagus tips on six serving plates and sprinkle over the spring onions. Gently spoon over the frothy sauce and serve at once.

# Open 'lasagne' of globe artichokes and Morel mushrooms with fresh herbs

This is a visually stunning dish that requires a little effort and care when assembling. You may be lucky enough to find fresh Morels in the woods on a guided mushroom foraging expedition, or you can purchase them fresh from local reputable fungi suppliers such as those listed on page 284.
Serves 6

For the artichokes & pasta:
6 large globe artichokes
1 lemon, halved
*Pasta...*
225g/ 8oz '00' pasta flour
2 tbsp chopped mixed garden herbs
5 free-range egg yolks
1 whole free-range egg
2 tbsp extra virgin olive oil

For the Morel filling:
200g/ 7 oz fresh or dried Morels
150g/ 5 oz baby spinach leaves, washed
150g/ 5 oz Parmigiano Reggiano
Handful of fresh herbs
2 tbsp toasted pine nuts
15g/ ½ oz unsalted butter

For the dressing:
100ml/ 3 ½ fl oz extra virgin olive oil
25ml/ 1 fl oz cider vinegar
1 tsp wholegrain mustard
Juice of ½ lemon

Sea salt & black pepper

For the pasta:
1. Sift the flour with the seasoning into a large bowl, making a well in the centre. Add the egg yolks, oil and herbs and bring the ingredients together with a wooden spoon. When the pasta dough has come together, *knead* it for 5-10 minutes until smooth. Wrap in Clingfilm and chill for 1 hour.
2. On a lightly floured surface, divide the pasta in half and roll it out to make 1-2mm thickness sheets. If you have a pasta machine then gradually roll the pasta through the machine until you have the thinnest sheets possible. Chill these pasta sheets for 15 minutes and then cut the pasta into eighteen discs approximately 8cm/ 3″ in diameter. Place on a very lightly floured surface and reserve in the fridge until required.

For the artichokes:
1. Prepare a large pan of salted water with half of the lemon squeezed into it.
2. Using a large sharp knife cut the artichokes about 5cm/ 2″ above the stem (Fig.1).
3. Cut away the long stalk leaving about 2 ½ cm/1″ at the base of the globe (Fig.2).
4. Peel off the tough outer leaves and trim the artichoke and stalk with a small knife to leave a smooth round disc and stalk resembling an inside-out umbrella (Fig.3).
5. Rub the artichokes with the remaining half of the lemon to prevent them turning brown.
6. Scoop out the hairy choke using a small spoon or melon baller (Fig.4). Place the artichokes in the pan of salted and acidulated water.

7. Bring the artichokes to the boil and then simmer for about 10-12 minutes or until just tender. Cool in the cooking liquid.

For the Morel filling and the dressing:
1. If you are using dried Morels, you will need to soak them in warm water for 1 hour before use. After soaking, clean the Morels with a small brush and cut in half.
2. Heat the butter in a small frying pan and sauté the Morels for 2-3 minutes. Season and keep warm.
3. To prepare the dressing, whisk together the vinegar, mustard and lemon juice. Gradually whisk in the olive oil and season to taste.
4. Peel the cheese into thin shavings using a potato peeler.

To finish and serve:
1. Bring a large pan of salted water to the boil and blanch the pasta discs for 1 minute. Drain and coat lightly with a dash of olive oil. Keep warm.
2. Remove the artichokes from the cooking liquid and cut each into six equal pieces.
3. On six serving plates, place a disc of pasta in the centre and then arrange three pieces of artichoke, some Morels, spinach leaves and cheese shavings. Add another disc of pasta and repeat the layering. Finish with the final disc of pasta. Garnish with the herbs and drizzle with the dressing. Sprinkle with the pine nuts and serve.

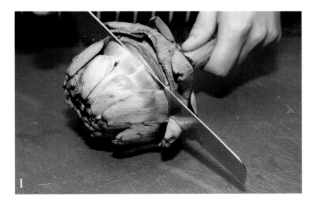
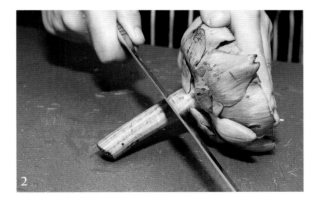

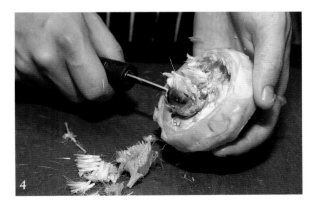

"As cooks, we have the right to enhance or heighten flavours, but we do not have the right to destroy them"

(*Joel Robuchon, Cuisine Actuelle*)

# Mixed salad of garden lettuces and herbs with olive oil and lemon

An opportunity to use all those tender young salad leaves and herbs you have nurtured. Be sure to use the freshest lemon and fruitiest olive oil for a crisp, zesty salad.
Serves 6

750g/ 1lb 9oz mixed garden lettuces
Large handful of mixed herbs
Small handful nasturtium petals
6 spring onions
100ml/ 3 ½ fl oz extra virgin olive oil
Grated *zest* & juice of 1 lemon
Sea salt & black pepper

*Chefs tip*
*Dress the salad just before serving because the acidity from the lemon will start to break down and wilt the lettuce leaves if left to stand. The idea is to enjoy a delicately flavoured crisp salad.*

1. Wash, drain and carefully tear each lettuce into bite-sized pieces. Gently combine in a large bowl.
2. Wash, drain and carefully pick the leafy herbs, removing the stalks. Snip the chives into 3cm/ 1″ lengths.
3. Cut the spring onions into fine *julienne*.
4. Mix the lettuce, herbs and spring onions together and then divide into six serving bowls.
5. Whisk together the olive oil and lemon juice then season to taste.
6. Dress the salad with the olive oil and then sprinkle with the nasturtium. Serve.

# Crispy herb risotto with lettuce parcels, lettuce sauce and herb oil

This requires a little more time and preparation but the effort is well worth it. Pungent herbs in the creamy risotto combine well with the light lettuce sauce. *Panko* breadcrumbs can be purchased from your local Oriental supermarket and they enhance the risotto cakes with a beautiful light, crisp coating.
Serves 6

For the risotto:
1lt/ 1 ¾ pints vegetable stock (see basics)
1 medium onion, finely chopped
1 garlic clove, peeled & finely crushed
250g/ 9oz Carnaroli risotto rice
150ml/ 5 fl oz white wine
100g/ 3 ½ oz Parmigiano Reggiano
2 tbsp crème fraîche
2 tbsp chopped mixed herbs
Juice of ½ organic lemon
150g/ 5oz Panko breadcrumbs
150g/ 5oz plain seasoned flour
2 beaten eggs

For the garnishes:
3 tbsp herb oil (see basics)
Sea salt & black pepper
Fresh herbs to garnish
3 tbsp olive oil

For the lettuce parcels:
1 large Iceberg or Cos lettuce
450g/ 1lb chestnut mushrooms, minced
1 medium onion, finely chopped
1 garlic clove, peeled & finely crushed
50ml/ 2 fl oz vegetable oil

For the lettuce sauce:
1 small Cos lettuce, washed & shredded
1 stick celery, thinly sliced
½ garlic clove, peeled & finely crushed
1 tbsp parsley, finely chopped
½ fresh bayleaf
200ml/ 7fl oz vegetable stock (see basics)
1 tbsp crème fraîche

To prepare the risotto:
1. Bring the vegetable stock to a simmer in a saucepan.
2. Heat the oil in a heavy based frying pan and *sweat* the onion and garlic together. Add the rice and fry for about 2 minutes, until the rice stops 'crackling'. Add the white wine and *reduce* by half. Begin to add the stock, one ladle at a time whilst stirring constantly. Once the stock has been absorbed into the rice, add another ladle of stock and so on. Repeat this for approximately 14-15 minutes until the rice is *al dente*.
3. Lower the heat and stir in the Parmigiano and then the crème fraîche. Cook for 1 minute.
4. Remove the pan from the heat and stir in the herbs and lemon juice. Season.
5. Transfer to a large shallow tray and chill as quickly as possible.
6. Once cold, form the risotto into eighteen evenly sized little cakes and chill again.

For the lettuce parcels:
1. Carefully separate the lettuce leaves and wash well. Cook in a steamer until just beginning to wilt. Remove and *refresh* in iced water, then drain and dry on kitchen paper or a clean tea towel.
2. Heat the oil in a frying pan and fry the onion and garlic until very lightly coloured. Add the mushrooms, increase the heat and fry for about 5 minutes until the mushrooms have softened. Season and drain the mushrooms of any excess liquor.
3. Once the mushrooms have drained, form them into six evenly sized balls.
4. Cut the lettuce leaves in suitable sizes and wrap the mushrooms tightly in a lettuce leaf. Reserve.

For the lettuce sauce:
1. Heat the butter in a medium saucepan and sweat the celery and garlic.
2. Add the shredded lettuce and cook until softened.
3. Add the vegetable stock and bring to a simmer with the parsley.
4. Stir in the crème fraîche and season.
5. Blend in a food processor until very smooth. Reserve.

To finish and serve:
1. '*Pane*' the risotto cakes by dusting in the flour, then dipping in the egg and finally coating in breadcrumbs.
2. Heat 3 tbsp of olive oil in a frying pan and gently *sauté* the risotto cakes on all sides until lightly golden.
3. Reheat the parcels in the steamer.
4. Reheat the lettuce sauce.
5. To serve, spoon some lettuce sauce and herb oil onto the warmed serving plates and arrange three risotto and three lettuce parcels on the sauces. Garnish with extra sprigs of fresh herbs and serve.

Crispy herb risotto with lettuce parcels, lettuce sauce and herb oil

Light salad of radish, tarragon, orange, cashews and olive oil

# Light salad of radish, tarragon, orange, cashews and olive oil

This would make an ideal little side salad to accompany some sautéed lightly spiced prawns. Simply *sauté* some fresh shelled prawns in a little groundnut oil and add a pinch of dried chilli flakes, ground coriander, cumin and ginger. Garnish with some freshly chopped coriander.
Serves 6

350g/ 12oz radishes
6 large sweet organic oranges
2 baby gem lettuces, washed & broken into small pieces
75g/ 2 ½ oz organic cashew nuts, toasted
1 tbsp tarragon leaves, washed
50ml/ 2fl oz extra virgin olive oil
Sea salt & black pepper

1. Wash, top then tail and thinly slice the radishes.
2. Peel and segment the oranges and squeeze any remaining juice from the orange into a small mixing bowl.
3. In a large bowl, combine the radishes, lettuce, cashews, tarragon and orange segments.
4. Whisk together the orange juice and olive oil and season to taste.
5. Gently toss into the salad.
6. Divide between six small serving bowls and serve.

# Aromatic duck salad with marinated young beetroots

This is a very visually attractive dish. The spices balance the rich duck and the balsamic vinegar adds sweetness to the beetroot and salad. Be sure to rest the duck breasts for at least 10 minutes after cooking to prevent the juices escaping when you slice the meat. Beetroot is one of my favourite ingredients, and here I have used the 'Burpees Golden', 'Chioggia Pink' and 'Boltardry' varieties. Remember to wear an apron when preparing beetroots as they are prone to 'bleeding'.

Serves 6

For the duck breasts:
4 free-range duck breasts
½ tsp ground cinnamon
½ tsp ground cumin
½ tsp ground fennel seeds
½ tsp ground coriander
½ tsp dried crushed chilli

Sea salt & black pepper

For the marinated beetroots:
450g/ 1lb assorted young beetroots
3 tbsp extra virgin olive oil
2 tbsp aged/vintage balsamic vinegar

For the garnish:
150g/ 5oz mixed fine leaf salad leaves

For the beetroot:
1. Peel the beetroots and slice them thinly to an approximate thickness of 2mm.
2. Place the beetroot in a single layer on a shallow tray.
3. Whisk the oil and balsamic vinegar together and brush evenly over the beetroot.
4. Season with salt and pepper and leave to *marinate* for 1 hour.

For the duck:
Pre-heat the oven to 220°C/ 425°F/ Gas mark 7
1. Trim the duck breasts of any silver skin and sinew and then score the fat in a criss-cross fashion.
2. Combine the spices and work them into the duck breasts. Season the meat and leave to *infuse* for 15 minutes.
3. Heat a non-stick frying pan and when it's very hot, seal the duck breasts fat side down. Continue to cook the duck like this for a good 6-7 minutes. Remove any fat from the pan periodically. (This renders down the fat and helps to give a thin and crispy skin).
4. Remove the duck and place on a roasting tray.
5. Cook in the oven for 3-4 minutes.
6. Remove and *rest* for 10 minutes and then slice each breast into twelve thin slices.

To finish and serve:
1. On six serving plates, arrange an overlapping circle of beetroot and then do the same with the duck slices, leaving a small gap in the centre of the plate.
2. Place a small pile of salad leaves in the centre and drizzle over any extra beetroot marinade. Serve.

Aromatic duck salad with marinated beetroots

# Spring cabbage and Thai rice rolls
# with chilli and lemongrass stock

This is a Thai inspired dish making good use of tender spring cabbage from the kitchen garden. Thai food offers a multitude of flavours that seamlessly blend together in harmony, and the vast majority of Thai cooking is based around rice. This would make a fabulous vegetarian starter as well as integrating itself into a full Thai meal.
Serves 6

For the Thai rice rolls:
200g/ 7oz Thai glutinous rice
2 tsp coriander leaves, chopped
6 spring onions, chopped
75g /2 ½ oz peanuts or cashews, crushed
12 large spring cabbage leaves, washed

For the vegetable garnish:
6 small young carrots, washed & sliced
100g/ 3 ½ oz bean sprouts
2 tbsp fresh coriander leaves

Toasted sesame oil
Sea salt & black pepper

For the chilli & lemongrass stock:
300ml/ 11fl oz vegetable stock (see basics)
1 fresh red chilli, seeded & finely chopped
2 sticks fresh lemongrass, coarsely chopped
1 garlic clove, peeled & crushed
small piece of galangal root, grated
1 tsp root ginger, peeled & finely chopped
2 cardamom pods
1 star anise
1 tsp coriander seeds

For the spring cabbage:
1. Prepare the rice as per packet instructions. This will invariably involve soaking the rice and then steaming it.
2. Once the rice is cooked, cool, and then mix in the spring onions, coriander and nuts. Season.
3. *Blanch* the cabbage leaves in boiling salted water for 30 seconds. *Refresh* in iced water, drain and dry the leaves on a clean tea towel.
4. Lay out a cabbage leaf on a bamboo mat and place some rice onto the leaf. Roll up the cabbage and form into a neat spring roll shape. Repeat this to make twelve rolls. Chill.

For the chilli and lemongrass stock:
1. Combine all the ingredients in a saucepan and simmer for 20 minutes. Pass through a fine sieve into a clean pan and add the sliced carrots. Simmer until the carrots are just cooked and then add the bean sprouts and coriander. Season to taste.

To finish and serve
1. Reheat the cabbage rolls in a steamer. Place the cabbage rolls into six serving bowls and spoon over the stock.
2. Brush the cabbage rolls with a little toasted sesame oil to give them a glossy shine to them. Serve.

# Wild sea trout and prawns baked 'en papillote', with broad beans and marjoram, broad bean sauce

This dish gives you the opportunity to present individual parcels at the table where you and your guests can open them and immediately experience the cooking aromas and vivid colours.
Serves 6

For the parcels:
6 pieces 30cm sq/ 12″ sq greaseproof paper
25g/ 1oz melted butter
6 x 200g/ 7oz fillets of skinless & boneless wild sea trout
300g/ 10oz peeled & de-veined fresh prawns
300g/ 10oz podded broad beans
1 tbsp marjoram leaves
18 small baby shallots, peeled
150ml/ 5fl oz vegetable stock (see basics)
150ml/ 5fl oz white wine
6 tsp extra virgin olive oil
Grated *zest* & juice of 1 organic lemon

For the sauce:
1 medium onion, finely chopped
½ garlic clove, crushed
1 tbsp vegetable oil
150g/ 5oz podded broad beans
300ml/ 11fl oz vegetable stock
(see basics)
3 tbsp crème fraîche

Sea salt & black pepper

For the sea trout parcels:
Pre-heat the oven to 200°C/ 400°F/ Gas mark 6
1.  *Blanch* the broad beans and shallots in boiling salted water for 90 seconds and *refresh* in iced water. Drain. Shell the broad beans.
2.  Dampen the sheets of greaseproof paper with water and lay them out on a work surface. Brush the outer inch of the paper with the melted butter.
3.  Divide the shallots and broad beans and pile just below centre of the paper. Lay the sea trout on top of these vegetables. Arrange the prawns around the fish. Sprinkle with marjoram and lemon zest and then divide the wine and stock around the fish. Season.
4.  Fold over the paper and then fold and seal the open edges to form a neat sealed parcel.
5.  Transfer to a lightly greased baking tray. Chill until required.

For the sauce:
1.  In a medium pan, heat the oil and *sweat* the onion and garlic until soft.
2.  Add the broad beans and cook for 2 minutes. Add the vegetable stock and simmer for 5 minutes. Whisk in the crème fraîche and season.
3.  Blend in a food processor until smooth. Chill until required.

To finish and serve:
1.  Place the parcels in the oven and bake for 12-15 minutes. After this, the parcels should have risen nicely and the fish be just cooked.
2.  Reheat the sauce and pour into a sauceboat.
3.  To serve, place the parcels on the plates and present to your guests. Once they have torn open the parcels, pour in the sauce.

# Pesto crusted new season lamb with basil cous cous and baby vegetables

This dish has a real Mediterranean feel to it. The pesto crust provides a good contrast in flavour to the lamb and it also provides more colour to the finished dish. As well as the tender spring lamb, the baby vegetables are a real highlight. The amazing sweet taste of freshly picked or dug baby vegetables is really evident. This is a good opportunity to reap the rewards of your effort in growing and tending your produce.
Serves 6

18 lean noisettes of new season lamb (each weighing about 30g/ 1 ½ oz)
2tbsp olive oil

For the pesto crust:
50g/ 2oz basil leaves
50ml/ 2fl oz olive oil
2 tsp pine nuts
1 garlic clove, peeled
2 tsp grated Parmigiano Reggiano
100g/ 3 ½ oz fresh granary breadcrumbs

For the basil cous cous:
500ml/ 18fl oz hot vegetable stock (see basics)
150g/ 5oz cous cous
50g/ 2oz basil leaves, finely chopped
1 tbsp extra virgin olive oil

450g/ 1lb washed, prepared & steamed baby vegetables of your choice
Fresh green & opal basil leaves to garnish
Sea salt & black pepper

For the pesto crust:
1.   Using a pestle and mortar, mix the basil leaves, olive oil, pine nuts, garlic and parmesan cheese together until smooth. Mix in the breadcrumbs and season. It should form into a soft savoury 'dough'.

For the cous cous:
1.   Heat the vegetable oil and gently fry the cous cous for 1 minute.
2.   Add the hot stock, cover and leave to stand for 7-8 minutes.
3.   Stir in the chopped basil and season. Keep warm.

To finish and serve:
Pre-heat the grill.
1.   Coat the lamb lightly in the olive oil and season well. Arrange on a non-stick shallow baking tray and grill under a high heat for 2 minutes on each side. Spoon a little of the pesto crust onto each noisette and *gratinate* until the crust is golden.
2.   Re-heat the vegetables in the steamer.
3.   Re-heat the cous cous gently.
4.   On six warmed plates, arrange three small piles of cous cous and sit a noisette of lamb on each.
5.   Arrange the vegetables attractively and drizzle with olive oil. Serve.

# New season spring lamb with its miniature suet pudding and new season vegetables

I like to prepare this dish just after Easter time as it uses typically spring produce in the form of spring lamb, asparagus and purple sprouting broccoli. The little suet puddings are meltingly tender and you could prepare them the day before along with the sauce, to save time during the final preparation of the dish. If you don't have any onion compote to hand, then you can substitute it with two onions that have been peeled, sliced and sautéed until lightly coloured.
Serves 6

For the spring lamb and miniature suet puddings:
1 best end of spring lamb, weighing about 2kg/ 4 ¼ lb
450g/ 1lb lamb neck fillet
1 medium onion, peeled & roughly chopped
1 garlic clove, peeled & crushed
200ml/ 7fl oz white wine
2 sprigs of thyme & rosemary
2 tbsp vegetable oil
300g/ 10oz organic plain flour
150g/ 5oz beef suet
1 tsp thyme leaves
3 tbsp onion compote (page 208)
50g/ 2oz unsalted butter
Sea salt & black pepper

For the vegetables:
18 stems of asparagus
250g/ 9oz purple sprouting broccoli
100ml/ 3 ½ fl oz herb oil (see basics)

For the sauce:
Lamb bones from best end
1 large onion
1 large carrot
2 sticks celery
1 leek
1 bouquet garni
1 tbsp tomato puree
4 lts/ 5 pints water

*Chefs tip!*
*Form a loyal relationship with*
*your butchers and I'm sure they*
*will prepare the lamb for you*
*if you are a little unsure about it.*

To prepare the lamb:
1. Remove the loins from the best end of lamb. Carefully cut away any sinew and silver skin. Refrigerate the lamb loins.
2. Remove any excess fat from the best end and chop the bones into 5cm/ 2″ pieces.

To prepare the sauce:
1. Heat a large saucepan and add the chopped lamb bones. Pan roast over a high heat until browned. Drain the bones on kitchen paper and remove most of the fat from the pan.
2. Wash and roughly chop the vegetables and add to the pan. *Sauté* over a high heat until well coloured.
3. Add the lamb bones and water and stir in the tomato puree. Add the bouquet garni.
4. Bring to the boil, *skim* and reduce to a simmer. Cook for 3 hours, skimming regularly.
5. Strain the stock through a fine sieve and return to a clean pan. *Reduce* to a quantity of approximately 500ml/ 18 fl oz. Season and reserve.

To prepare the suet puddings:
1. Heat 1 tbsp of the vegetable oil in a saucepan and add the neck fillet. Sauté until lightly coloured and then add the garlic and onion. Cook for a further minute and add the wine. Reduce by half and then cover with water. Add the sprigs of thyme and rosemary. Place a lid on the pan.
2. Bring to the boil, temporarily remove the lid, skim and reduce the heat to a simmer. Return the lid.
3. Cook for 1 hour then leave the lamb to cool in the liquid.
4. Meanwhile, combine the flour, suet and herbs in a mixing bowl and season.
5. Mix together well and add enough cold water to form a smooth even dough. Chill for 15 minutes.
6. Grease six small individual Dariole moulds.
7. Roll the dough out to an even thickness of 2-3mm. Cut out circles and line the Dariole moulds. Cut six pastry lids the same size as the top of the Dariole mould and reserve.
8. Remove the lamb from the cooking liquid. Cut off any excess fat or sinew and cut the lamb into 1cm/ ½″ cubes. Place in a bowl, season and stir in the onion compote.
9. Divide and press the lamb into the Dariole moulds. Add the pastry lid and press the edges to seal them.
10. Wrap the moulds in tin foil and steam for 3 hours. Keep warm in a low steamer or chill until required.

To prepare the vegetables:
1. Wash, trim and steam the asparagus and broccoli until just tender. *Refresh* in iced water, drain and reserve.

To finish and serve:
Pre-heat the oven to 220°C/ 425°F/ Gas mark 7
1. Heat 1 tbsp of vegetable oil in a large frying pan. Season the lamb loins and sauté in the oil, turning regularly for 8-10 minutes. Remove and *rest* for at least 5 minutes.
2. Reheat the suet puddings if needed and remove from the moulds using a thin, long knife.
3. Reheat the vegetables and sauce.
4. Cut the lamb into eighteen even slices and arrange three of these on each of the six warmed serving plates. Place a suet pudding in the centre of the plate.
5. Garnish with the vegetables and pour the sauce around.
6. Drizzle with herb oil and serve.

New season spring lamb with it's miniature suet pudding and new season vegetables

# Steamed wild salmon wrapped in sorrel, served with baby pak choi and piquant tomato sauce

A small amount of sorrel gives salmon a lovely lemony flavour. However, if you don't grow or cannot buy sorrel you could substitute with basil or even spinach. To accompany this dish you could serve some new potatoes cooked with a little mint and dressed in extra virgin olive oil.
Serves 6

For the salmon:
6 x 200g/ 7oz fillets skinless & boneless wild salmon
12-18 sorrel leaves

For the tomato sauce:
250g/9oz ripe tomatoes, roughly chopped
1 garlic clove, peeled & finely crushed
1 medium onion, finely chopped
1 tbsp olive oil
3 tbsp red wine vinegar
½ tsp demerara sugar
150ml/ 5fl oz vegetable stock (see basics)
Dash of Tabasco sauce
2 sprigs of thyme, rosemary & oregano
50g/ 2oz unsalted butter
6 small heads of baby pak choi, washed
Sea salt & black pepper

*Chefs tip*
*Salmon is a really versatile ingredient.*
*Marinating, steaming, poaching in a*
*flavoured stock, or sautéing all work well.*
*Oily fish, such as salmon, are high in Omega*
*3 fatty acids; so are therefore essential in a*
*healthy balanced diet.*

For the tomato sauce:
1. Using a medium saucepan, heat the olive oil and then *sweat* the onion and garlic.
2. Add the tomatoes and cook for 3 minutes. Add the vinegar and the sugar and cook for a further 2 minutes. Add the vegetable stock and bring to a simmer.
3. Add the herbs, Tabasco and simmer for a further 10 minutes.
4. Remove from the heat and season. Blend in a food processor until very smooth and then pass through a fine sieve to remove any seeds. Keep the sauce warm over a low heat.

For the salmon:
1. Season the fish and wrap two or three sorrel leaves around the middle of each fillet. Place in steamer and cook for 6-8 minutes. Fresh salmon is best served slightly under-cooked to prevent it being dry.

To finish and serve:
1. After the salmon has been cooking for 4 minutes, add the heads of baby pak choi to the steamer. Once they have wilted/softened and the salmon is cooked, remove and place onto six serving plates. Whisk the butter into the sauce without boiling it and then spoon the sauce around the salmon and serve.

Steamed wild salmon wrapped in sorrel, served with baby pak choi and piquant tomato sauce

The fish market

# Herb roasted fillet of beef with wild garlic, Morels and crispy new season potatoes

A beef fillet that has been aged for a minimum of twenty one days and then cooked with lots of herbs and garlic is enough to get most people eagerly anticipating the result. Take interest in the provenance of the beef you purchase; ask your butcher which farm it was reared on, what it was fed on and what breed the animal was (my preference is Dexter, Charolais, Limousin or Aberdeen Angus). Wild garlic can be found alongside rivers and in damp woodland during the spring and summer months. Quickly blanched it imparts a light garlic flavour through the dish without being overpowering. Spring cabbage, peas or sprouting broccoli would be an ideal accompaniment to this recipe.
Serves 6

For the beef fillets:
Approximately 1kg/ 2lb 2oz centre cut beef fillet
2 tbsp vegetable oil
Handful of thyme, rosemary & sage leaves
1 garlic clove, crushed
50g/ 2oz unsalted butter

For the sauce:
1 large onion
1 garlic clove, crushed
1 bottle red wine
1 tbsp redcurrant jelly
500ml/ 18fl oz beef stock (see basics)

For the garnishes:
300g/ 10oz Morel mushrooms
A handful of fresh wild garlic shoots, washed (spring onions will suffice as a substitute)
450g/ 1lb small even sized new season potatoes
3 tbsp olive oil

Sea salt & black pepper

To prepare the beef:
  1. Wrap the beef fillet very tightly in several layers of Clingfilm and chill in the fridge.

To prepare the sauce:
  1. Peel and roughly chop the onion and garlic.
  2. Place in a saucepan and add the red wine and redcurrant jelly.
  3. Bring to the boil and *reduce* by three quarters.
  4. Add the beef stock and reduce by a further three quarters.
  5. Pass through a fine sieve, season and reserve.

To prepare the garnishes:
  1. Rinse and scrub the Morels well to remove any soil.
  2. Wash the potatoes and simmer in salted water until just tender. Refresh, drain and cut into even sized rounds about 5mm/ ¼" thick. Reserve.

To finish and serve:

Pre-heat the oven to 220°C/ 425°F/ Gas mark 7

1. Heat 2 tbsp of vegetable oil in an ovenproof frying pan (all metal, no plastic handle).
2. Cut the beef fillet into six even steaks, leaving the Clingfilm attached around its circumference.
3. Season the beef and fry on each side for 3 minutes over a high heat.
4. Add the herbs and butter and coat the beef in the resulting herb glaze.
5. Transfer the pan to the oven and cook for between 3 (rare) and 10 (well done) minutes.
6. Remove, take off the Clingfilm and *rest* the beef for at least 10 minutes.
7. Heat 2 tbsp of the olive oil in a frying pan and *sauté* the potato slices until golden. Season and reserve.
8. *Blanch* the wild garlic for 20 seconds in a pan of boiling water and reserve.
9. Heat 1 tbsp of the olive oil in a frying pan and sauté the Morels until lightly coloured. Season and reserve.
10. Re-heat the sauce.
11. To serve, re-heat the beef in the oven for a minute or two and then place in the centre of the plate. Garnish with the potatoes, wild garlic and Morels, then spoon over some sauce.

Herb roasted fillet of beef with wild garlic, Morels and crispy new season potatoes

Thai monkfish curry with baby vegetables and Thai rice wrapped in lettuce

# Thai monkfish curry with baby vegetables and Thai rice wrapped in lettuce

This is one of my personal favourites. I love the spicy, sweet but slightly salty curry, as well as the sticky coriander rice wrapped in lettuce. You should be able to find all the spices in your local Oriental supermarket or even the larger supermarkets. It's probably best to experiment with the strength of the curry paste to find the level of heat that suits you best.
Serves 6

For the curry paste:
2 long red chillies, de-seeded
1 stick lemongrass, chopped
1 star anise
1 tsp minced Thai basil
2 tsp palm sugar

1 garlic clove, peeled
1 tsp coriander seeds
5g/ ¼ oz cinnamon sticks
10g/ ½ oz galangal root
200ml/ 7fl oz coconut milk

10g/ ⅓ oz root ginger, peeled
1 tsp cumin seeds
3 cardamom pods
2 tsp fish sauce
200ml/ 7fl oz vegetable stock

For the Thai rice:
200g/ 7oz Thai glutinous rice
2 tsp coriander leaves, finely chopped
12 medium iceberg lettuce leaves

For the garnishes:
2 tbsp toasted peanuts
1 tbsp coriander leaves, finely chopped
750g/ 1lb 9oz mixed baby vegetables

750g/ 1lb 9oz cleaned and skinned monkfish tail
Sea salt

*Chefs tip*
*Raw or pickled vegetables, and fresh watermelon are also ideal accompaniments to this Thai curry.*

To prepare the curry paste:
1. Using a pestle and mortar or a food blender, puree the chillies, garlic, ginger, lemongrass, coriander, cumin, star anise, cardamom, cinnamon, basil and galangal together. Mix in the fish sauce.

To prepare the Thai rice:
1. Follow the instructions on the packet to cook your rice. This will invariably involve soaking the rice and then steaming it. Once the rice is cooked, mix in the coriander and season.
2. *Blanch* the lettuce leaves in boiling salted water for 30 seconds. Remove, *refresh* in iced water, then drain and dry on a clean tea towel.
3. Divide the rice, wrap in the lettuce leaves and form into balls. Reserve.

To prepare the baby vegetables:
1. Steam the vegetables individually and refresh in iced water. Drain and reserve.

To prepare the monkfish curry:
1. Cut the monkfish into 3cm/ 1″ cubes. Season and steam for 6 minutes. Remove and reserve.
2. Mix the curry paste with the vegetable stock in a wok and cook over a medium heat for about 10 minutes. This is called 'frying' the curry paste. When the paste is almost dry, stir in the palm sugar and cook until it begins to caramelise. Add the coconut milk and cook for 2 minutes.
3. Add the monkfish and carefully combine. Season and reserve.

To finish and serve:
1. Re-heat the lettuce balls and the vegetables in the steamer.
2. Re-heat the curry and serve in shallow serving bowls. Serve the rice and vegetables in separate small serving dishes and sprinkle the curry with the peanuts and coriander. Serve.

# Herb omelette with caramelised baby onions and smoked salmon

Omelettes are not difficult to prepare providing you have a good non-stick pan and fresh eggs. I would serve this for a spring lunch or supper dish accompanied by a mixed garden leaf salad or perhaps tomato and chilli chutney.
Serves 2

6 free-range organic eggs
2 tbsp vegetable oil
25g/ 1oz unsalted butter

12 baby onions, peeled & halved
1 tbsp vegetable oil
½ tsp demerara sugar

200g/ 7oz best quality organic smoked salmon

2 tbsp mixed herbs, washed & stalks removed
Sea salt & black pepper

For the onions:
1.  Heat the oil in a non-stick frying pan and fry the onions until lightly golden. Add the sugar and caramelise the onions. Season and reserve.

For the omelette:
1.  Crack the eggs into two bowls (three in each). Lightly beat with a fork and season.
2.  Heat two small non-stick frying pans and divide the oil and butter between each.
3.  Add the eggs and stir over a medium heat. Once the egg starts to scramble, press down into the base of the pan and cook for a minute. Remove from the heat. The omelette should still look slightly runny. This is called '*baveuse*'.
4.  Lay the smoked salmon over half the omelette and then fold over the other half using a fish slice or palette knife.
5.  Transfer to a serving plate and spoon the onions around. Garnish with the mixed herb leaves and serve.

# Vanilla marshmallow meringue with wild strawberries and chocolate peppermint

Wild strawberries are a delight. They originate from one of the American wood strawberries and are believed to have arrived in Europe in the early 1600's. Here, they are served with crisp and soft meringue and an unusual mint that imparts a delicate chocolate overtone to the dessert.
Serves 6

4 large free-range organic egg whites
200g/ 7 oz castor sugar
Pinch of salt
1 tsp cornflour
1 vanilla pod, seeds scraped out
1 tsp vanilla extract
1 tsp lemon juice

350g/ 12oz fresh wild or similar strawberries
200ml/ 7 fl oz double cream, lightly whipped

Handful of chocolate peppermint leaves, torn

For the meringue:

Pre-heat the oven to 140°C/ 275°F/ Gas mark 1
1. Whisk the egg whites until voluminous (fig.1).
2. Gradually pour in the sugar (fig.2) and whisk until you can stand a spoon up in it (fig.3).
3. Add the vanilla seeds and extract, lemon juice and cornflour and mix well.
4. Line a baking tray with silicon paper.
5. Using a piping bag, pipe the meringue into six walnut whip shapes of equal size (fig.4).
6. Bake in the oven for about 45 minutes until the outside of the meringue is pale and crisp to the touch. The middle should still be moist (but not runny). Test by inserting a thin knife into base of the meringue.
7. Wash and *hull* the strawberries.
8. Carefully cut the meringues in half and spoon in a little whipped cream and some of the strawberries. Sprinkle half the mint on top. Place the meringue hat back on top.
9. Use a little cream to stick the meringues to the serving plates, garnish with the remaining strawberries and mint. Serve.

The Essence - Contemporary recipes inspired by a traditional kitchen garden

Vanilla marshmallow meringue with wild strawberries and chocolate peppermint

# Salad of strawberries
# with aged balsamic vinegar and basil

This is a marriage of flavours that really enhance the strawberries. Perfect for when you have unexpected guests.
Serves 6

750g/ 1lb 9oz washed & *hulled* fresh strawberries
12 basil leaves
3 tbsp 15 year-old balsamic vinegar

To serve:
1. 20 minutes before serving, simply combine the strawberries and balsamic vinegar in a bowl.
2. Arrange the strawberries on a serving dish and just tear the basil leaves and sprinkle over. Serve.

Strawberry and champagne jelly with lavendar crème fraîche

# Strawberry and champagne jelly
# with lavender crème fraîche

You will need six tall slender glasses for this recipe. This is an elegant dessert for a spring or early summer dinner party. You could serve with freshly baked shortbread.
Serves 6

250g/ 9oz ripe strawberries, washed & *hulled*
100g/ 3 ½ oz castor sugar
250ml/ 9fl oz apple juice
250ml/ 9fl oz water
250ml/ 9fl oz pink champagne, good quality
6 gelatine leaves, soaked in cold water until soft

6 small perfect strawberries
3 lavender flowers, broken into petals
100g/ 3 ½ oz crème fraîche

For the jelly:
1. In a heavy saucepan, boil together the sugar, apple juice and water. *Reduce* by a quarter. Chill.
2. Once cold, puree with the strawberries in a blender. Pass through a fine sieve to remove any seeds.
3. Drain the gelatine and melt in a small pan over a low heat. Mix into the strawberry liquid. Chill.
4. Once the jelly has begun to set, gently pour in the champagne and mix well.
5. Pour into the glasses and chill in the fridge until completely set.

To finish and serve:
1. Remove the jellies from the fridge 10 minutes before you need them.
2. Mix the lavender flowers into the crème fraîche.
3. Spoon a little crème fraîche on top of the jelly and finish with a strawberry. Serve.

# Assiette of strawberries

'Assiette' used in this context refers to a plate of small individual desserts. Some extra effort is needed here, but you should find that the finished result reflects the quality of your strawberries as well as giving the 'wow' factor. You will need to prepare the parfait and sorbet the day before.
Serves 6

For the parfait:
175g/ 6oz free-range organic egg yolks
150g/ 5oz castor sugar
2 tsp vanilla extract
3 gelatine leaves, soaked in cold water until soft
100g/ 3 ½ oz crème fraîche
250ml/ 9fl oz double cream, whipped to soft peaks
150g/ 5oz free-range organic egg whites
50g/ 2oz castor sugar

For the vanilla tuiles:
25g/ 1oz softened unsalted butter
Seeds from 1 vanilla pod
25g/ 1oz icing sugar
25g/ 1oz organic plain flour
25g/ 1 oz free-range organic egg white

For the strawberry sauce:
50ml/ 2fl oz water
juice of ½ lemon
100g/ 3 ½ oz strawberries, washed
50g icing sugar

For the strawberry sorbet:
500ml/18fl oz water
250g/ 9oz castor sugar
200g/ 7oz strawberries, washed

For the garnish:
24 strawberry crisps (see page 77)
24 small strawberries
12 edible garden flowers

To prepare the parfait:
1. Put the sugar in a heavy based saucepan with 2 tbsp water. Heat slowly to 120°C/ 237°F (use a sugar thermometer to judge the temperature).
2. Meanwhile, using an electric mixer, whisk the egg yolks and vanilla until pale. Then, trickle in the sugar whilst still hot and continue to whisk until cool.
3. Drain the gelatine and melt over a low heat.
4. Whisk in the gelatine.
5. Fold in the crème fraîche, followed by the double cream.
6. In a separate bowl, whisk the egg whites and sugar to soft peaks and then fold into the egg mix.
7. Divide the mixture between Clingfilm lined ramekins or round moulds and freeze.

To prepare the sorbet:
1. Combine the water and sugar in a heavy based pan, bring to the boil and reduce by a quarter. Chill.
2. When cold, add the strawberries, liquidise, pass through a fine sieve and churn in the sorbet machine. Freeze.

To prepare the vanilla tuiles:

1. Combine all the ingredients in a mixing bowl and mix until smooth and homogeneous (even). Chill the mix for 1 hour.
2. Pre-heat the oven to 200°C/ 400°F/ Gas mark 6.
3. Make a template in the shape of your choice using a spare plastic lid (e.g. triangular or circular). Place the template on a *silpat* or sheet of silicon paper. Spread the mixture over the template aperture to reveal your chosen shape in tuile mixture. Repeat to make twelve shapes. Bake in the centre of the oven until lightly golden brown. Remove from the oven and carefully transfer the tuiles to a cooling rack.

To prepare the strawberry sauce:

1. Combine all the ingredients and blend in a processor until smooth. Pass through a sieve and chill until required.

To finish and serve:

1. Arrange as per photograph or in a similar fashion if you desire.

# White chocolate parfait
# with strawberry compote and crisps

You will need a 450g/ 1lb loaf tin lined with Clingfilm for this recipe. Here, you have three contrasting but complimentary textures; the iced parfait, the soft strawberry compote and then the strawberry crisps. Food should awaken as many senses as possible, and the different textures within a dish can really bring it to life.
Serves 6

For the parfait:
175g/ 6oz free-range organic egg yolks
100g/ 3 ½ oz castor sugar
3 gelatine leaves, soaked in cold water until soft
150g/ 5oz melted white chocolate
1 tsp vanilla extract
350ml/ 12fl oz double cream

450g/ 1lb small to medium ripe strawberries
100g/ 3 ½ oz large slightly under-ripe strawberries
2 tsp chopped mint leaves
1 tbsp toasted flaked almonds

6 mint leaves to garnish

For the crisps:
Heat the oven to 110°C/ 225°F/ Gas mark ½.
1.  Wash, *hull* and pat dry the large strawberries. Cut into 2mm thick slices.
2.  Arrange the slices on a *silpat* or silicon paper and place on a baking tray in the oven.
3.  Bake for about 2 ½ hours until crisp. You can test the slices by removing one onto a cold surface. If it crisps up straight away then they are ready. Once the strawberries are crisp, store them in an airtight container.

Recipe continued overleaf.

To prepare the parfait:

1. Put the sugar in a heavy based pan and add 1 tbsp of cold water. Heat slowly to 120°C/ 237°F (Use a sugar thermometer to judge the temperature). Remove from the heat and cool the pan slightly in a sink of cold water to stop the cooking process.
2. Whilst the sugar is cooking, whisk the egg yolks until pale using an electric whisk and then slowly trickle in the hot sugar. Continue to whisk until cool.
3. Drain the gelatine and melt over a low heat with a dash of water.
4. Whisk the gelatine into the eggs and then fold in the white chocolate and vanilla extract.
5. Whisk the cream to soft peaks and fold into the eggs and chocolate.
6. Transfer the parfait mix to the lined loaf tin and freeze until firm.

To prepare the *compote*:

1. Wash, hull and dry the smaller strawberries.
2. Heat a large frying pan over a medium heat. Add the strawberries and toss in the pan for 1 minute until they have softened slightly. Transfer to a bowl and chill.

To finish and serve:

1. Remove the parfait from the freezer 10 minutes before you serve it.
2. Combine the strawberry compote with the chopped mint leaves and the toasted almonds.
3. Using a hot knife, which will aid you in achieving a smooth surface, slice the parfait equally into six slices.
4. Place the parfait onto chilled serving plates and place a spoonful of the compote on the side. Arrange the crisps by sticking them into the parfait itself and then garnish with mint and serve.

Strawberry slices and strawberry crisps

White chocolate parfait with strawberry compote and crisps

# Rhubarb and blood orange tart with lavender ice cream and cinnamon butterscotch sauce

Fresh puff pastry is needed here. You can readily buy this in many supermarkets, but I have also listed a recipe for puff pastry in the Basics & Condiments chapter on page 268. This dessert is particularly suitable for early spring when the first of the forced rhubarb appears and when blood oranges are readily available.
Serves 6

For the ice cream:
250ml/ 9fl oz organic milk
250ml/ 9fl oz organic double cream
1 tsp vanilla extract
2 tsp crushed lavender petals
6 free-range organic egg yolks
150g/ 5oz castor sugar

For the rhubarb and orange tart:
6 sticks tender pink rhubarb
3 large blood oranges
300g/ 10oz fresh puff pastry (see basics)
1 free-range egg yolk
100g/ 3 ½ oz castor sugar

For the cinnamon butterscotch:
200ml/ 7fl oz organic double cream
50g/ 2oz demerara sugar
25g/ 1oz unsalted organic butter
½ tsp ground cinnamon

For the garnish:
6 fresh mint or lemon balm leaves
Ground cinnamon

To prepare the ice cream:
1. In a heavy based saucepan, heat the milk, cream, lavender and vanilla to boiling point.
2. Meanwhile, whisk the egg yolks and the sugar together until pale in a heatproof bowl.
3. Pour the boiling milk and cream onto the eggs and whisk together.
4. Return to the heat in a clean pan and cook over a low heat, stirring constantly, until the liquid begins to thicken. Once it is of a consistency to coat the back of a spoon, remove from the heat and cool the pan immediately over ice.
5. Once cold, pass through a fine sieve and churn in an ice cream machine. Freeze.

To prepare the butterscotch sauce:
1. Combine the ingredients in a heavy based saucepan and cook over a medium heat, stirring frequently, until the sauce has *reduced* by half. The result should be a rich, thick creamy sauce. Reserve.

To prepare the rhubarb tart:

Pre-heat the oven to 200°C/ 400°F/ Gas mark 6.

1. Roll out the pastry on a lightly floured surface to an even thickness of 3mm/ ⅛″.
2. Cut out six 10cm/ 4″ circles and '*dock*' the middle 8cm/ 3 ½ ″ of the circle with a fork. Chill the circles for 15 minutes.
3. Wash and dry the rhubarb and remove any blemishes. Cut each stick into 2cm/ ¾ ″ slices.
4. Wash and grate the *zest* from the oranges and then peel and segment them.
5. Remove the pastry circles from the fridge and place on a lined or non-stick baking tray.
6. Arrange the rhubarb slices neatly around the pastry leaving a 1cm/ ½″ gap around the edge.
7. Sprinkle with the orange zest and the sugar.
8. Place in the centre of the oven and cook for about 15 minutes until the pastry has risen around the edges and the rhubarb has softened and slightly caramelised. Sprinkle the orange segments on top of the rhubarb and return to the oven for another 5 minutes.

To finish and serve:

1. Warm the butterscotch sauce.
2. Place the tarts onto the serving plates and spoon a little sauce around the tart.
3. Place a ball or *quenelle* of ice cream on the tart and garnish with some mint or lemon balm sprigs and a dusting of ground cinnamon. Serve.

Rhubarb and blood orange tart with lavender ice cream and cinnamon butterscotch sauce

# Gooseberry mousse with Woodruff jelly and sweet orange oat biscuits

The gooseberry season begins with those small green fruit that are ideal for cooking. They impart their delicate sweet flavour into jellies, mousses, syllabubs and compotes perfectly. Later in the season you can enjoy the deeper red coloured fruit which can be eaten raw in salads. Woodruff can be found growing around Beech trees and in damp woodland. It is traditionally added to wine and drinks and the leaves contain the enzyme coumarin which gives it a 'freshly mown hay' aroma. It is necessary to pick the woodruff the day before you require it, then, after it has wilted, it is refreshed in liquid where it imparts its own unique flavour. It is important not to consume woodruff in very large quantities on a regular basis as it may cause headaches.

Serves 6

For the gooseberry mousse:
450g/ 1lb gooseberries, washed & trimmed
100g/ 3 ½ oz castor sugar
250g/ 9oz fromage frais
4 gelatine leaves, soaked in cold water until soft
3 free-range organic egg whites
25g/ 1oz castor sugar

For the oat biscuits:
50g/ 2oz unsalted butter
1 tbsp organic clear honey
50g/ 2oz castor sugar
200g/ 7oz whole organic oats
Grated zest of 2 organic oranges
75g/ 2 ½ oz organic plain flour

For the Woodruff jelly:
10g/ ⅓ oz Woodruff, rinsed & then wilted overnight
500ml/ 18fl oz fresh pure apple juice
Juice of 2 organic oranges
5 gelatine leaves, soaked in cold water until soft

You will require six elegant glasses to present this dessert in.

To prepare the oat biscuits:
Pre-heat the oven to 190°C/ 375°F/ Gas mark 5
1. Dice the butter, then cream together with the sugar and clear honey.
2. Stir in the orange zest, oats and flour.
3. Add 2 tbsp of boiling water and bring the mix to a smooth, pliable dough.
4. Chill for 20 minutes.
5. Roll out the biscuit mix to an even thickness of 5mm/ ¼" and cut into rounds.
6. Transfer the biscuits to a lined or greased baking tray and bake in the oven for 10 minutes or until lightly golden.
7. Remove and cool the biscuits. Keep in an airtight tin until required.

To prepare the gooseberry mousse:
1. Place the gooseberries and 100g/ 3 ½ oz of castor sugar into a saucepan, cover and simmer over a medium heat until the gooseberries have softened.

2. Transfer the fruit to a blender and puree until smooth. Pass through a fine sieve and then chill the gooseberry puree.
3. Once completely chilled, stir in the fromage frais.
4. Drain and melt the gelatine in a saucepan over a low heat and stir into the fruit puree.
5. Whisk the egg whites with the 25g/ 1oz of castor sugar to soft peaks and fold into the fruit puree.
6. Spoon into the glasses and tap the glasses to ensure the mousse is as level as possible.
7. Transfer the glasses to the fridge and chill until set.

Meanwhile, prepare the Woodruff jelly:
1. Combine the apple juice, orange juice and Woodruff in a pan and bring to a simmer.
2. Remove from the heat and leave to *infuse* for 45 minutes, then pass through a fine sieve.
3. Drain the gelatine and melt in a pan over a low heat. Stir the melted gelatine into the liquid and chill until it just begins to set.
4. Gently pour the Woodruff jelly onto the mousses and then return to the fridge to set before serving with the orange oat biscuits.

A lunch prepared in honour of the gardener's

The Essence - Contemporary recipes inspired by a traditional kitchen garden

# Summer

I have classified summer as June through to mid September, but again, as our climate changes and the seasonal temperatures and hours of sunshine vary, this is just a guide. Summer will no doubt provide the beginning of the 'glut' of produce from your kitchen garden or vegetable patch, as well as offering a plentiful selection on farmers' stalls and in markets.

A busy time for the gardener and home cook alike, the summer months offer an abundance of fruit, salads and vegetables as well as beautifully aromatic herbs. The aforementioned are suitable for preserving, jam making and freezing as well as immediate consumption. I believe that in most cases, freezing fruit and vegetables can be an effective way of storing excess produce instead of recycling it onto the compost heap.

Summer obviously lends itself to light, fresh and vibrant cooking. The recipes in this chapter reflect that – fantastic food for the terrace or patio.

You can enjoy recipes involving the following produce in this chapter: new season potatoes, tomatoes, peas, courgettes, aubergines, spinach, chard, onions, herbs, raspberries, figs, cherries, apricots, peaches, plums and edible garden flowers.

Simple summer gazpacho soup

# Simple summer gazpacho soup

What could be better than sitting down to a bowlful of fresh, vibrant and piquant Gazpacho soup? Adorn this soup with nothing but olive oil and crusty ciabatta bread.
Serves 6

15 large, ripe, juicy tomatoes
1 small red onion or shallot, finely chopped
½ garlic clove, peeled & finely crushed
1 tbsp red wine vinegar
1 tsp demerara sugar
½ tsp Tabasco sauce
Juice of ½ lemon
Sea salt & black pepper
1 cucumber cut into 5mm/ ¼ ″ cubes
3 spring onions cut into 5mm ¼ ″ slices
6 basil leaves, shredded finely
6 large mint leaves, shredded finely
Extra virgin olive oil

1. Roughly cut the tomatoes and liquidise in a food blender until smooth. Pass the tomatoes through a fine sieve, pressing the pulp well to extract all of the juice and goodness. Chill.
2. In a small saucepan, combine the onion or shallot, garlic, vinegar and sugar. Simmer gently over a low heat until the onion just begins to soften. Cool.
3. In a large bowl, combine the tomato juice with the onions, cucumber, spring onions, lemon juice and Tabasco sauce.
4. Season to taste.
5. Spoon into chilled serving bowls and sprinkle on the basil and mint.
6. Drizzle with the olive oil and serve.

# Pressing of vine tomatoes and Buffalo mozzarella with red and green basil, tomato coulis

This dish requires a little patience in its preparation and assembly. I would recommend that you start the preparation at least 12 hours before you want to serve it, as the pressing needs some time to set and gel together. As a garnish, I suggest fresh basil mayonnaise or herb oil.
Serves 6

For the pressing:
18 large deep red ripe tomatoes
450g/ 1lb Buffalo mozzarella (large pieces)
12 large leaves of opal basil
12 large leaves of green basil
1 tbsp black olive *tapenade*

For the tomato coulis:
6 large deep red tomatoes
1 tbsp red wine vinegar
1 tsp demerara sugar

For the basil mayonnaise:
25ml/ 1fl oz white wine vinegar
4 black peppercorns
½ bayleaf
2 free-range egg yolks
200ml/ 7fl oz groundnut oil
Juice of ½ lemon
8 large leaves of green basil

Sea salt & black pepper

You will need a 450g/ 1lb loaf tin lined with Clingfilm.

To prepare the pressing:
1. Bring a large pan of water to the boil.
2. Wash the tomatoes and cut out the core.
3. Have a bowl of iced water ready, and then *blanch* the tomatoes for approximately 30 seconds. The skins should just be beginning to peel off. *Refresh* the tomatoes in the iced water, then drain and pat dry. Peel off the tomato skins carefully.
4. Halve the tomatoes and remove the seeds. Lay the tomato shells out on kitchen paper and press flat to dry.
5. Slice the Buffalo mozzarella into 1cm/ ½ ″ thick slices and season with salt and pepper.

6. Place a neat layer of mozzarella in the base of the loaf tin and top with tomatoes. Arrange some basil leaves on top of tomatoes, then a thin layer of the olive tapenade, and then repeat the process twice more. Finish with a neat layer of mozzarella.
7. Cover with Clingfilm and place a suitable sized weight, such as two bags of flour, on the top of the tin. This creates the 'pressing' effect. Place in the fridge and chill for at least 12 hours.

To prepare the tomato coulis:
1. Roughly cut the tomatoes and then puree in a blender until smooth. Add the red wine vinegar, sugar and season to taste. Pass through a fine sieve and chill.

To prepare the basil mayonnaise:
1. In a small saucepan, *reduce* the vinegar together with the peppercorns and bayleaf by half. Pass through a sieve and cool.
2. Whisk the egg yolks with the vinegar until pale and frothy.
3. Slowly trickle in the groundnut oil, whisking constantly.
4. Using a pestle and mortar, puree the basil to a fine paste.
5. Mix the basil and lemon juice into the mayonnaise and season to taste. Reserve.

To finish and serve:
1. Remove the pressing from the fridge and slice carefully into six. You will find it easier to slice the pressing whilst it is still wrapped in the Clingfilm.
2. On the serving plates, make a decorative pattern on one side of the plate with the basil mayonnaise.
3. Place a slice of the pressing on the mayonnaise. Drizzle a tiny amount of olive oil on the pressing and brush over the surface evenly. Sprinkle with a little sea salt.
4. Spoon some tomato coulis next to the pressing and serve.

# Tomato risotto with basil marscapone and aged balsamic vinegar, toasted pine nuts

An Italian inspired dish that offers a different slant on a classical combination of ingredients. The higher the standard of balsamic vinegar you use, the better the quality of the finished dish. Of the three types of risotto rice available (Arborio, Carnaroli and Vialone) I prefer to use Carnaroli - it retains a nice 'al dente' bite as well as helping to produce a creamier risotto.
Serves 6

For the risotto:
2 tbsp olive oil
1 medium onion, finely chopped
1 garlic clove, peeled & finely crushed
200g/ 7oz Carnaroli risotto rice
200ml/ 7fl oz dry white wine
1 lt/ 1 ¾ pints vegetable stock (see basics)
50g/ 2oz grated Parmigiano Reggiano cheese
25g/ 1oz unsalted butter, diced
2 tbsp chopped chives

For the tomato:
10 ripe Red Alert or Roma tomatoes
1tbsp extra virgin olive oil

Sea salt & black pepper

For the basil marscapone:
100g/ 3 ½ oz marscapone cheese
100g/ 3 ½ oz basil leaves

For the garnish:
Small handful mixed herbs
Small handful mixed lettuce
2 tsp extra virgin olive oil
2 tbsp 15 year-old balsamic vinegar
75g/ 2 ½ oz organic pine nuts, toasted

To make the tomato puree for the risotto:
1. Wash and roughly chop the plum tomatoes. Place in a saucepan and cook over a medium heat until most of the liquid has evaporated and you have a thick tomato sauce. Season and add the olive oil.
2. Puree in a food blender and pass through a fine sieve to remove any seeds. Reserve.

To prepare the basil marscapone:
1. Using a pestle and mortar, grind the basil leaves to a fine paste.
2. Fold into the cheese, season and chill.

To prepare the garnishes:
1. Wash, dry and remove the stalks from the herbs and salad. Pick into small pieces and chill.

To make the risotto:

1. Bring the vegetable stock to boiling point in a saucepan and then leave to simmer.
2. Meanwhile, heat the olive oil in a large, shallow, heavy based frying pan.
3. Add the garlic and onion and fry gently (fig.1).
4. Add the risotto rice and 'fry' until the rice stops 'crackling'.
5. Add the white wine and reduce by half (fig.2).
6. Begin to add the stock, one ladleful at a time. Stir the risotto constantly whilst continuing to add the stock (fig.3).
7. Once the rice is '*al dente*' (approximately 14 minutes from first adding the stock), remove from the heat and stir in the Parmigiano cheese (fig.4) and then the butter. Fold in the tomato puree and season.

To finish and serve:

1. Using six ring moulds or cookie cutters, spoon the risotto into the moulds in the centre of the serving plates.
2. Spoon some balsamic vinegar around the risotto.
3. Place a spoonful or *quenelle* of basil marscapone on the risotto.
4. Lightly toss the herbs and lettuce leaves with olive oil and sprinkle over the plate.
5. Finish with the toasted pine nuts and serve.

"If you are a chef, your life is devoted to giving pleasure to other people. We are creative, and what we create is gone almost instantly; but there is always the thought that maybe tomorrow we will create something even better"

(*Anton Mosimann, The Art of Anton Mosimann*)

# Baked fresh Borlotti beans
# with slow roasted Roma tomatoes and lemon basil

This is an excellent alternative to baked beans and traditional soups. It can be made with the minimum of fuss, and is great served with some crusty French bread and perhaps some Italian salami or Parma ham. Roma tomatoes are a variety of plum shaped tomatoes, but Tigerella tomatoes will work just as well.
Serves 6

For the baked Borlotti beans:
450g/ 1lb podded Borlotti beans
2 tbsp olive oil
1 medium red onion, sliced
4 sticks celery, washed & peeled
1 garlic clove, peeled & finely crushed
200ml/ 7fl oz white wine
500ml/ 18fl oz vegetable stock (see basics)
1 bayleaf
2 tbsp organic tomato puree
1 tbsp chives, finely chopped

For the roasted tomatoes:
12 large Roma tomatoes
1 tbsp balsamic vinegar
1 tbsp olive oil
1 tsp thyme leaves
½ garlic clove, peeled & finely crushed

Handful of lemon basil leaves
Sea salt & black pepper
Extra virgin olive oil

To make the baked Borlotti beans:
Pre-heat the oven to 180°C/ 350°F/ Gas mark 4.
1. In an ovenproof saucepan (no plastic handles), heat the olive oil, and then gently *sauté* the onion, garlic and celery over a medium heat.
2. Add the Borlotti beans and cook for 1 minute.
3. Add the wine and *reduce* by half.
4. Pour on the vegetable stock, and then stir in the tomato puree.
5. Add the bayleaf, season, cover and transfer to the oven. Cook for approximately 1 hour, until the beans are tender and have absorbed most of the liquid. Remove the bayleaf.

Meanwhile, prepare the tomatoes:
Pre-heat the oven to 140°C/ 275°F/ Gas mark 1.
1. Core and halve the tomatoes. In a bowl, combine the tomatoes with the garlic, vinegar, olive oil and thyme leaves. Season, and then arrange in a single layer in a baking tray.
2. Place at the bottom of the oven and cook for about 40 minutes, until the tomatoes are soft but still holding their shape. Remove and reserve.

To finish and serve:
1. Fold the roasted tomatoes, including the cooking juices into the Borlotti beans and check the seasoning.
2. Spoon into deep serving bowls and sprinkle with torn lemon basil leaves. Drizzle with some of the extra virgin olive oil and serve.

# New season baby potato salad
# with watercress and horseradish

This salad really emphasises the quality and taste of new season potatoes. By combining them with the heat and acidity of the horseradish and lemon, along with the peppery, irony watercress you create a well-balanced salad that would partner grilled beef or chicken very well. Horseradish is actually native to Asia but is now commonly found growing throughout Europe. The root can grow up to 50cm/ 1 ½ feet long and after scraping the skin away, it is grated before using as a condiment. It can be combined with soured cream or mayonnaise, which reduces the heat.

Serves 6

1kg/ 2lb 2oz evenly sized new season baby potatoes
250g/ 9oz watercress, washed
1 tbsp prepared horseradish sauce or 2 tsp freshly grated horseradish
Juice of 1 lemon
2 tbsp extra virgin olive oil
Sea salt & black pepper

1. Wash and scrub the potatoes and place in a saucepan of salted water.
2. Bring to the boil and then simmer until they are cooked (insert a thin knife into the middle of the potato; if the potato falls away from the knife easily, it is cooked).
3. *Refresh* the potatoes in iced water and then drain.
4. Slice the potatoes into 1cm/ ½" thick slices and season. Reserve.
5. Pick the watercress into bite sized pieces removing any woody stalks.
6. In a bowl, whisk together the olive oil, lemon juice and horseradish. Season.
7. On six serving plates, arrange a neat circle of the potato slices and top with a neat pile of watercress. Spoon over some of the horseradish dressing and serve.

# Warm salad of new season potatoes with dwarf beans and crispy ham

This salad is given a new dimension by the dressing made with sherry vinegar and walnut oil. Both of these impart their own unique flavour. This is a quick and easy salad to prepare and one that you could comfortably start 30-40 minutes before lunch or dinner.
Serves 6

For the salad:
450g/ 1lb evenly sized new season potatoes
350g/ 12oz dwarf beans, top & tailed
150g/ 5 oz sliced Parma or Serrano ham
100g/ 3 ½ oz baby spinach leaves, washed
6 button onions, peeled & thinly sliced

For the dressing:
2 tbsp sherry vinegar
1 tsp Dijon mustard
6 tbsp walnut oil
1 tbsp baby capers

Sea salt & black pepper

1. Wash and scrub the potatoes. Place in a saucepan of salted water, bring to the boil and then simmer until cooked. Drain and cool slightly.
2. Slice the potatoes into 1cm/ ½″ thick slices, season and keep warm.
3. Bring a large pan of salted water to a fast boil and cook the dwarf beans until just tender. Drain and keep warm.
4. Cut the ham slices into 1cm/ ½″ strips. Heat a non-stick frying pan over a high heat and dry fry the ham until crispy. Drain on kitchen paper and reserve.
5. Whisk together the vinegar and mustard. Whisk in the walnut oil. Season and add the capers.
6. To serve, arrange the potatoes, spinach and beans in six serving bowls. Sprinkle with sliced onions and spoon over some dressing.
7. Warm the ham and sprinkle over the salad. Serve.

# Nettle gnocchi with watercress and blue cheese sauce

Stinging nettles invariably grow in most gardens, and they thrive in soil that is nitrogen and phosphate rich. Cooking the nettles destroys their sting, but remember to wear strong gloves when picking them. The young top leaves are best for culinary purposes, therefore spring and early summer is the best time to prepare this recipe. Gnocchi is a typically Italian dish, and the nettles give a nice nutty flavour as well as a summery colour.
Serves 6

For the nettle gnocchi:
250g/ 9oz nettle leaves
850g/ 1lb 14oz large floury potatoes
250g/ 9oz organic plain flour
1 free-range organic egg
Pinch of grated nutmeg
50g/ 2oz unsalted butter

Organic plain flour for dusting
Sea salt & black pepper

For the blue cheese sauce:
1 medium onion, peeled & finely chopped
1 garlic clove, peeled & finely crushed
200ml/ 7fl oz organic whole milk
50ml/ 2 fl oz double cream
150g/ 5oz gorgonzola cheese

For the garnish:
100g/ 3 ½ oz freshly grated Italian hard cheese
200g/ 7oz fresh watercress

To prepare the gnocchi:
Pre-heat the oven to 200°C/ 400°F/ Gas mark 6
1. Wash, prick and bake the potatoes in the oven until soft.
2. Meanwhile, *blanch* the nettles in boiling salted water for 1 minute. *Refresh* in iced water, drain and finely chop. Reserve.
3. Scoop out the potato from the skins and mash with a fork. Next, pass the mashed potato through a sieve. Mix it with the flour, egg, nutmeg, butter and chopped nettles whilst still hot. Season to taste. Transfer to a piping bag with a 1 ½cm/ 1" plain nozzle and pipe out long sausages of the potato mix. Cut each sausage into 4cm/1 ½ " lengths. Dust the gnocchi in flour and press each one with a fork to make an indentation. Reserve the gnocchi on a floured surface while you make the sauce.

To prepare the blue cheese sauce:
1. Combine the onion, garlic, milk and cream in a saucepan and bring to a simmer for 10 minutes. Add the cheese, transfer to a blender and puree until smooth. Season and keep warm at a very low heat.

To finish and serve:
1. Bring a large pan of salted water to the boil.
2. Add the gnocchi to the water and gently simmer until the gnocchi rise to the surface.
3. Drain the gnocchi into serving bowls and spoon over the blue cheese sauce.
4. Sprinkle with the grated cheese, some chopped parsley and a drizzle of olive oil. Add a turn of black pepper and serve.

# Textures of courgettes with goat's cheese, lemon, Nasturtiums and Hemerocallis flowers

This is a pretty and fragrant dish. If you prefer not to eat goats' cheese then you could substitute it for a firm creamy cheese such as Vignotte or Brillat-Savarin. Here I am using a tempura of courgette flowers to give extra texture and crispiness. The flowers provide vivid colour as well as another sweet and perfumed aspect to the dish.
Serves 6

Principal ingredients:
450g/ 1lb long courgettes (yellow & green)
6 small round courgettes
350g/ 12oz mature, firm goats' cheese
1 organic un-waxed lemon
4 tbsp extra virgin olive oil
1 tbsp white wine vinegar
Handful of nasturtium & Hemerocallis petals
6 spring onions
1 tbsp snipped chives

For the *tempura*:
10 courgette flowers
100g/ 3 ½ oz cornflour
25g/ 1oz plain flour
½ tsp bicarbonate of soda
½ tsp baking powder
300ml/ 11fl oz sparkling water
Approx 1lt/ 1 ¾ pints vegetable oil

Sea salt & black pepper

To prepare the principal ingredients:
1. Wash then top and tail the courgettes.
2. Peel half of the long courgettes into long ribbons using a potato peeler. Cut the other half into 2cm/ ¾" cubes. Cut the top centimetre of the round courgette and hollow out the middle using a melon baller. Return the tops and steam the round courgettes until tender.
3. Wash and cut the spring onions into 1cm/ ¼" slices. Cut the cheese into 2cm/ ¾" cubes.
4. Grate the *zest* of the lemon, extract the juice and combine the zest and the juice with 3 tbsp of the olive oil and the vinegar. Season and reserve.

To prepare the tempura:
1. Heat the oil to 180°C/ 350°F.
2. Mix the flours, bicarbonate of soda and baking powder together. Using a fork, lightly mix in the sparkling water and season.
3. Remove the stamen (centre bud) from the flowers and split the flowers in two.
4. Dip the flowers into the tempura batter and then carefully drop them into the oil, a few at a time. Fry until they are crisp and golden brown. Remove and drain on kitchen paper.

To finish and serve:

1. Heat 1 tbsp of olive oil in a frying pan and fry the courgette cubes until lightly coloured.
2. Meanwhile combine the long ribbons of courgette with the lemon dressing and season.
3. Place half of the courgette cubes in the six round courgettes and reheat these in a steamer. On six serving plates, arrange courgette ribbons, the round courgette, the remaining courgette cubes and the goats' cheese attractively.
4. Garnish with the courgette flower tempura, the chives, the Hemerocallis and nasturtium petals and drizzle over any remaining lemon dressing. Serve.

# Chilled courgette and avocado soup with quail eggs

A really simple and easy to make soup finished with soft-boiled quail eggs. These are quite unusual and novel but are becoming more readily available as a fresh product as well as being also sold lightly pickled in jars.
Serves 6

450g/ 1lb green courgettes, finely sliced
2 tbsp olive oil
1 medium onion, finely chopped
1 garlic clove, peeled & finely crushed
1 lt/ 1 ¾ pints vegetable stock (see basics)
3 tbsp crème fraîche
3 medium, ripe organic avocados
Juice of ½ organic lemon
225g/ 7oz baby spinach leaves
18 fresh quail eggs
100ml/ 3 ½ fl oz white wine vinegar
Snipped chives
Sea salt & white pepper

1. Heat the olive oil in a deep saucepan and *sweat* the onion and garlic until softened.
2. Add the courgettes and cook for a further 6-8 minutes.
3. Add the stock, bring to the boil and then simmer for 20 minutes.
4. Puree in a food blender until smooth and then chill.
5. Peel, stone and roughly chop the avocados and mix with the lemon juice.
6. Add this mixture to the courgette soup along with the spinach leaves and crème fraîche. Blend again. Then pass through a fine sieve. Chill.
7. Bring a large pan of salted water to the boil and cook the quail eggs for 2 minutes and 50 seconds. Plunge into iced water immediately and add the vinegar.
8. After about 20 minutes you will notice the eggs appearing to peel themselves. Drain and remove the shell carefully and then rinse gently.
9. Season the soup and divide between six chilled serving bowls. Garnish with three quail eggs and sprinkle with snipped chives. Serve.

# Grilled red mullet with saffron and crunchy fennel salad

Red Mullet is predominately available during the summer and autumn months and is readily caught off the Devon and Cornish coast and in the Bay of Biscay. You should be able to source it from your local fishmonger, even if you have to pre-order it. Red mullet has a good meaty flesh and quite a rich flavour. Here, I've combined it with saffron and a crunchy fennel salad that provides a good contrast in texture. You could serve it with a simple salad such as the one on page 38, or new potatoes finished with chopped parsley and olive oil.
Serves 6

6 red mullet (approx 300g/ 10oz each), scaled, cleaned, filleted & boned
A pinch of saffron strands
4 tbsp olive oil
2 small fennel bulbs
1 tbsp chopped dill
Juice of ½ organic lemon
Handful of picked herbs such as chervil, dill, coriander & chives
Sea salt & black pepper

Pre-heat the grill to a medium to high heat.
1. Wash and very finely slice the fennel. Combine with 2 tbsp of the olive oil, the lemon juice and the dill. Season and reserve.
2. Rub an equal amount of saffron onto the skin of the red mullet fillets and leave to marinate for 5 minutes.
3. Arrange the fillets on a non-stick tray and drizzle with olive oil. Season.
4. Grill the red mullet for 6-8 minutes until the flesh is just firm and the skin slightly crispy.
5. Remove the fish to six serving plates and garnish with the fennel salad.
6. Drizzle any remaining fennel dressing over the dish and sprinkle with the herbs. Serve.

Grilled red mullet with saffron and crunchy fennel salad

Baked aubergine "Lucas Carton style" with herb cous cous and marinated tomatoes

# Baked aubergine "Lucas Carton style" with herb cous cous and marinated tomatoes

This recipe was inspired by my stage [*training period*] at the 3 Michelin star restaurant, Lucas Carton, in Paris. The Chef Patron, Alain Senderens, is a world class chef with an enviable eye for detail. I learnt much during my training there, including this fabulous aubergine recipe which everybody has loved. The secret lies in the deep caramelising of the aubergine and in the time spent reducing the sauce. Although the whole dish would be a wonderful accompaniment for lamb, it is substantial enough to be a stand alone main course. It would be best to start the tomatoes 4 hours in advance.
Serves 6

For the aubergine:
6 medium to large aubergines
100ml/ 3 ½ fl oz vegetable oil
2 tbsp brown sugar
200ml/ 7fl oz balsamic vinegar
200ml/ 7fl oz full-bodied red wine
½ tsp ground coriander
500ml/ 18fl oz vegetable stock (see basics)
100ml/ 3 ½ fl oz double cream

Handful of mixed herbs to garnish
Sea salt & black pepper

For the herb cous cous:
250g/ 9oz cous cous
3 tbsp olive oil
500ml/ 18fl oz chicken stock (see basics)
2 tbsp chopped mixed herbs
Juice of ½ organic lemon

For the marinated tomatoes:
6 large ripe plum tomatoes
½ garlic clove, peeled & finely crushed
1 tsp thyme leaves
2 tbsp olive oil

To prepare the tomatoes:
  1. Wash, core and quarter the tomatoes. Remove the seeds and combine with the garlic, thyme leaves and olive oil and leave to marinate at room temperature for 4-6 hours.

To prepare the aubergines:
  1. Wash, top and tail, and cut each aubergine into three equal lengths of about 6cm/ 2 ½".
  2. Heat the oil in a large heavy based frying pan until just smoking.
  3. Fry the aubergines in the oil until very caramelised but not burnt. Turn them regularly to ensure even cooking.
  4. Once they are heavily coloured, drain off any excess oil and add the sugar. Caramelise the sugar and then add the balsamic vinegar. *Reduce* by half whilst coating the aubergines.
  5. Add the red wine and reduce by half again.
  6. Next, add the chicken stock, coriander and double cream. Season and reduce the heat to a simmer.
  7. Continue to reduce the sauce, turning the aubergines occasionally.
  8. The result should be a rich, deeply coloured sauce, whilst the aubergines should have softened and absorbed the cooking sauce. Adjust the seasoning and keep warm.

To prepare the cous cous:
1. Bring the stock to the boil.
2. In a separate pan, heat the olive oil and gently fry the cous cous for 1 minute.
3. Add the stock; remove from the heat and leave to stand for 6-7 minutes.
4. Stir again with a fork and mix in the lemon juice and chopped herbs. Season.

To finish and serve:
1. Spoon the cous cous into the centre of the plates and place three aubergine pieces around it. Arrange some marinated tomatoes around the plate and finish with a few sprigs of mixed herbs. Serve.

# John Dory steamed with herbs,
## served with stuffed baby tomatoes and rocket sauce

John Dory is also known as St. Pierre or St. Peter's fish reputedly because in mythology St. Peter held the fish with his thumb and forefinger, thereby leaving a dark imprint on the fish's flesh. Myth or not, John Dory is a fantastic fish to cook, being of firm flesh, pearl white in colour with a rich, luxurious taste. I would recommend that you ask your fishmonger fillet the fish as John Dory has extremely sharp fins which can easily cause a nasty cut. Rocket is easy to grow and can be picked just eight weeks after sowing. It has a taste similar to mustard and watercress and is very 'en vogue'. It is excellent in salads, sauces and as flavouring to risotto and pesto.
Serves 6

For the John Dory & herbs:
3 John Dory (750g/ 1lb 9oz each), filleted & skinned
3 tbsp chopped herbs (basil, chives, lemon thyme)
Grated *zest* of 1 organic lemon
2 tbsp extra virgin olive oil
1lt/ 1 ¾ pints vegetable stock (see basics)
100ml/3 ½ fl oz white wine

For the rocket sauce:
450g/ 1lb fresh rocket, rinsed & roughly chopped
½ garlic clove, peeled & finely crushed
½ onion, peeled & finely chopped
1 tbsp olive oil
200m/ 7fl oz vegetable stock (see basics)
2 tbsp crème fraîche

Sea salt & black pepper

For the stuffed tomatoes:
18-24 baby Roma or cherry tomatoes
1 onion, peeled & finely chopped
1 garlic clove, peeled & finely crushed
3 tbsp basil leaves, finely chopped
100g/ 3 ½ oz fresh white breadcrumbs
3 tbsp olive oil

To prepare the stuffed tomatoes:
1. Heat 2 tbsp of the olive oil in a frying pan and *sweat* the onion and garlic until softened.
2. Remove from the heat and mix in the breadcrumbs and basil.
3. Season to taste.
4. Carefully cut three quarters of a slice off the top of the tomatoes leaving the top attached.
5. Scoop out the seeds from the tomato using a small spoon.
6. Stuff the tomatoes with the basil breadcrumbs.
7. Place on a baking tray and drizzle with 1 tbsp olive oil.

To prepare the John Dory and herbs:
1. Separate the fillets of the fish. Each side of the fish will naturally separate into three small pieces.
2. Arrange these pieces of fish into six equal portions.
3. Coat the upper side of the fillets in the olive oil and then in the herbs and lemon zest. Season the fish. Chill.

To prepare the rocket sauce:
1. Heat the olive oil in a saucepan and sweat the onion and garlic until softened.
2. Stir in the rocket and cook briefly.
3. Add the stock and bring to the boil.
4. Transfer to a blender and puree until very smooth.
5. Return to the pan, season and whisk in the crème fraîche. Keep warm at a very low heat.

To finish and serve:
Preheat the oven to 190°C/ 375°F/ Gas mark 5.
1. Fill a steamer with the vegetable stock and bring to the boil. Lay the fillets in the steamer trays and drizzle with white wine.
2. Steam the fish for 5-7 minutes depending on the size of the fillets.
3. Meanwhile, cook the tomatoes for 5 minutes in the oven and then *rest* for 2 minutes.
4. Reheat the sauce.
5. Place the fish onto six warmed serving plates and arrange the tomatoes next to the fish.
6. Spoon some rocket sauce around the fish and serve.

Poached lobster with baby spinach and chard, orange zest and sherry vinegar butter sauce

# Poached lobster with baby spinach and chard, orange zest and sherry vinegar butter sauce

Lobster is a luxurious ingredient, so therefore you should take the time to search out the freshest, best quality specimen you can. There are a number of schools of thought on the most humane way to kill a lobster. Personally, I prefer to store the lobster at a very cold temperature for a couple of hours in order to dull its senses before cutting straight through the 'cross' on its head in each direction. In this recipe, a sweet and sour style sauce marries well with the sweet succulent lobster flesh.
Serves 6

For the lobster & garnish:
6 x 450-600g/ 1-1 ¼ lb fresh live lobsters
200g/ 7oz baby spinach leaves, washed
350g/ 12oz young mixed chard, trimmed & washed
2 tbsp extra virgin olive oil
1 tbsp lemon juice
Sea salt & black pepper

For the sauce:
Grated *zest* & juice of 2 oranges
200ml/ 7fl oz sherry vinegar
2 tsp soft brown sugar
200ml/ 7fl oz white wine
100g/ 3 ½ oz unsalted butter, diced

To prepare the lobsters:
1. Bring a large pan of salted water to the boil.
2. Kill the lobsters as described above. Place in the boiling water (two at a time) and simmer for 8 minutes. Remove to a large bowl of iced water and repeat with the other lobsters.
3. Drain the lobsters and prepare as follows: separate the head from the tail (Fig.1) and separate the claws from the head (Fig.2). Split the head in half lengthways (Fig.3) and remove the stomach sack. Separate the knuckles from the main claw (Fig.4) and remove the meat. Crack the claw and remove the meat in one piece (Fig.5). Cut the underside of the tail section to remove the tail in one piece (Fig.6) and then remove the intestinal tract by making a shallow cut along the upper side (Fig.7). Arrange the lobsters on a baking tray as shown and cover with tin foil (Fig.8).

To prepare the sauce:
1. Combine the orange zest, juice, vinegar and sugar in a saucepan and reduce to a glossy syrup over a medium heat.
2. Add the white wine and *reduce* by half.
3. Turn the heat to low and gradually whisk in the diced butter. The result should be an *emulsified*, shiny sauce. Season and reserve at room temperature.

To finish and serve:
Pre-heat the oven to 180°C/ 350°F/ Gas mark 4

1. Bring a steamer of water to the boil.
2. Warm six large serving plates.
3. Warm the lobsters in the oven for 5-6 minutes.
4. Whisk together the olive oil and lemon juice and season.
5. Steam the chard leaves for 2 minutes and season.
6. Combine the spinach with the olive oil dressing.
7. Arrange the lobsters on the serving plates and spoon the chard around the lobster.
8. Garnish with the spinach.
9. Spoon over the sherry vinegar sauce and serve.

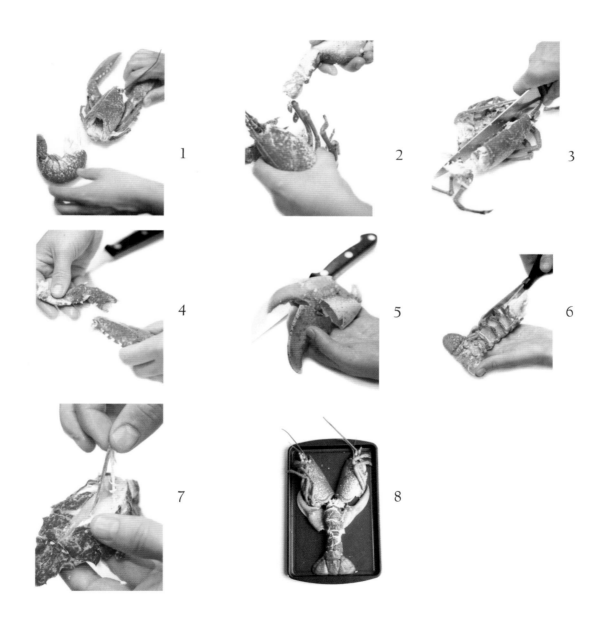

# Organic corn-fed chicken scented with lemon confit, crushed peas, crispy cured ham, Szechwan pepper dressing

Here I have used some lemon *confit* that is tucked between the chicken skin and flesh to give the meat a citrus kick. Freshly picked podded peas provide the backdrop, and a spicy Szechwan pepper dressing adds another vibrant flavour. We actually have a Szechwan pepper tree in the kitchen garden and it is particularly pleasing to be able to use fresh berries in our cooking.
Serves 6

For the chicken with lemon confit:
3 organic lemons
75g/ 2 ½ oz icing sugar
4 tbsp olive oil
1 tsp thyme leaves
6 breasts organic corn-fed chicken with skin
2 tbsp olive oil

For the garnishes and dressing:
6 slices cured ham, such as Parma or Serrano
50ml/ 2 fl oz sherry vinegar
2 tsp Dijon mustard
Juice of ½ organic lemon
2 shallots, peeled & very finely chopped
150ml/ 5 fl oz extra virgin olive oil
2 tsp crushed Szechwan pepper berries

For the crushed peas:
450g/ 1lb fresh peas
1 tbsp snipped chives
1 tsp marjoram leaves
50g/ 2oz salted butter
Juice of ½ lemon

Sea salt & black pepper

To prepare the lemon confit and chicken:
Preheat the oven to 140°C/ 275°F/ Gas mark 1.
  1. Peel the *zest* from the lemon in long strips.
  2. *Blanch* in boiling water and *refresh* in iced water. Drain and pat dry.
  3. Combine with the icing sugar, 4 tbsp of olive oil and the thyme leaves.
  4. Wrap in a tin foil parcel and place on a tray in the oven for 2 hours, or until the lemon is very soft and tastes both sweet and sour. Cool.

5. Increase the oven heat to 190°C/ 375°F/ Gas mark 5.
6. Make an opening between the chicken skin and flesh and place two or three strips of lemon confit in the gap. Replace the chicken skin and season.
7. Heat 2 tbsp of olive oil in a frying pan and fry the chicken breasts, skin side down first, for 4 minutes on each side. They should be lightly coloured.
8. Transfer to an ovenproof tray and cook in the centre of the oven for 10-12 minutes.
9. Remove from the oven and *rest* for 5 minutes.

Whilst the chicken is cooking and resting, prepare the peas and garnishes:
1. Heat a non-stick frying pan and dry fry the slices of cured ham until crispy. Drain on kitchen paper and reserve.
2. Dry roast the pepper berries in a frying pan until fragrant.
3. To make the dressing, whisk the vinegar, mustard, lemon juice and seasoning together. Stir in the shallots and then gradually whisk in the olive oil. Stir in the pepper.
4. Bring a pan of salted water to the boil and cook the peas for 3-4 minutes, until tender.
5. Drain and stir in the butter and lemon juice. Crush lightly with a fork and then stir in the chives and marjoram. Season to taste and reserve.

To finish and serve:
1. On six warmed serving plates, make a bed of crushed peas in the centre.
2. Slice each chicken breast into five slices and arrange on the peas.
3. Spoon some of the dressing around the chicken.
4. Cut the crispy ham into pieces and scatter over the chicken and serve.

**The Essence - Contemporary recipes inspired by a traditional kitchen garden**     123

# Herb roasted rump of veal with a fricassee of baby leeks, cauliflower and hazelnuts

Using veal which is animal-welfare friendly is an absolute must. The herbs really permeate the veal during cooking to leave it rich and aromatic. Be sure to wash your baby leeks very well as they are prone to harbouring soil. You could serve some crusty ciabatta, garlic bread or fresh pasta with this dish.
Serves 6

For the fricassee:
18 baby leeks, washed & trimmed
1 large or 2 medium cauliflower, washed
100g/ 3 ½ oz peeled hazelnuts
1 red onion, peeled & sliced
1 garlic clove, peeled & finely crushed
150ml/ 5fl oz dry white wine
200ml/ 7fl oz crème fraîche
2 tbsp snipped chives
6 chive flowers
2 tbsp olive oil
Sea salt & black pepper

For the rump of veal:
6 x 250g/ 9oz pieces of veal rump
2 sprigs of thyme, rosemary & sage
2 tbsp vegetable oil
25g/ 1oz unsalted butter

*Chefs tip*
*Hazelnuts can be peeled by toasting them under a hot grill, then rubbing them vigorously in damp tea towel to remove the skin.*

To prepare the fricassee:
1. Boil a large saucepan of salted water.
2. Cut the cauliflower into small florets and cook in the water until just tender. *Refresh* in iced water and drain.
3. Slice the leeks diagonally into 6cm/ 2 ½″ lengths.
4. In a large deep frying pan, heat the olive oil and sweat the red onion and garlic until soft.
5. Add the leeks and cook for 3-4 minutes. Add the cauliflower and hazelnuts and combine.
6. Next, add the white wine and *reduce* by half, then finish with the crème fraîche.
7. Simmer gently for a further 2-3 minutes, season and add the chives.

Meanwhile, prepare the rumps of veal:
Pre-heat the oven to 220°C/ 425°F/ Gas mark 7.
1. Season the pieces of veal rump - ensure that every inch is covered evenly.
2. In an ovenproof frying pan, heat the oil until very hot and then add the veal. Seal on all sides until golden brown and then add the herbs and butter.
3. Baste the veal all over with the juices and transfer to the oven for between 6 minutes (medium rare) and 12 minutes (well done). Once cooked, baste again with the cooking juices and then *rest* the meat for at least 10 minutes.

To finish and serve:
1. Re-heat the fricassee and spoon into six shallow warmed serving bowls.
2. Slice the veal and fan the slices over the fricassee. Sprinkle with chive flowers and serve.

# Rump of Yorkshire spring lamb with caramelised onion tart, pea and chorizo salad and goat's cheese

As you can see from the photograph this dish involves many vivid colours. The accompaniments to the lamb all have their own unique flavour, but they still unite beautifully with the tender sweet lamb. I use a muffin tray to cook the onion tarts.
Serves 6

For the onion tart:
6 medium red onions
100g/ 3 ½ oz castor sugar
25g/ 1oz unsalted butter
300g/ 10oz puff pastry (see basics)

6 small rumps of lamb (each weighing 250g/ 9oz)
1 tbsp vegetable oil
1 garlic clove, peeled & finely crushed
2 sprigs of thyme & rosemary
25g/ 1oz unsalted butter
200ml/ 7fl oz vegetable stock (see basics)
250g/ 9oz soft fresh goat's cheese

For the salad:
300g/ 10oz fresh peas
100g/ 3 ½ oz chorizo sausage
1 tbsp snipped chives
1 tbsp extra virgin olive oil

Sea salt & black pepper

To prepare the onion tart:
Pre-heat the oven to 200°C/ 400°F/ Gas mark 6.
1.  Peel the onions and slice off the top and root to leave an even sized centre of the onion about 3cm/ 1 ¼″ thick. You can use the onion trimmings for vegetable stock or a soup.
2.  In a heavy based pan, caramelise the sugar until it is a deep golden brown. Stir in the butter. Pour the caramel into the muffin trays filling them about half way. Place an onion centre on top of the caramel.
3.  On a lightly floured surface, roll out the puff pastry to an even thickness of 5mm/ ¼″. Cut out circles of pastry the same size as the muffin tray moulds.
4.  Press the pastry onto and around the onion slice.
5.  Cook in the oven for 25-30 minutes. The result should be a well caramelised onion and pastry edge. Remove from the tray and reserve.

To prepare the lamb:

Pre-heat the oven to 220°C/ 425°F/ Gas mark 7.

1. Season the lamb rumps all over.
2. Heat the oil in a large ovenproof frying pan. Once very hot, seal the lamb on all sides.
3. When the lamb is sealed all over, add the thyme, rosemary, garlic and butter. Baste the lamb with the resulting juices.
4. Transfer the lamb to an ovenproof dish and cook in the oven for 10-12 minutes (medium cooked).
5. Remove the lamb and *rest* the meat for at least 10 minutes.
6. Using the cooking dish, heat the cooking juices and herbs and add the vegetable stock. Boil for 2 minutes and then pass through a fine sieve. Reserve.

To prepare the salad:

1. Bring a saucepan of salted water to the boil. Add the peas, return to the boil and cook until tender. Drain and reserve.
2. Meanwhile, peel and thinly slice the chorizo sausage.
3. Heat a large non-stick frying pan and quickly fry the chorizo until crispy. Drain on kitchen paper.
4. Combine the peas with the chorizo, chives, olive oil and season. Keep warm.

To finish and serve:

1. Re-heat the onion tarts and place onto six warmed serving plates.
2. Slice the lamb and arrange next to the onion tart.
3. Add a spoonful of the peas and three small teaspoons of the goats' cheese to each plate.
4. Spoon some of the cooking liquor over the lamb and serve.

# Poached peaches with cinnamon and sweet wine sorbet

This is a simple dessert to make and one that will fill your kitchen with the wonderful aroma of cinnamon. The better quality of sweet wine you use, the better the quality of the sorbet. Peaches that are only just ripe would be perfect as you want them to retain their shape during the cooking.

Serves 6

For the poached peaches:
9 peaches
Water to cover
200g/ 7oz granulated sugar
2 cinnamon sticks

For the sweet wine sorbet:
500ml/ 18fl oz water
200ml/ 7fl oz sweet wine
200g/ 7oz granulated sugar
Juice of 1 organic lemon

3 sprigs of fresh mint or lemon balm leaves

To prepare the sorbet:
1. Bring the water and the sugar to the boil and *reduce* by a quarter.
2. Add the wine and lemon juice and chill.
3. Churn in a sorbet/ ice cream machine and then freeze until required.

To prepare the peaches:
1. Rinse, halve and stone the peaches. Place in a pan with the sugar and cinnamon and cover with the water.
2. Bring to a gentle simmer and poach the peaches until tender. Remove from the heat and leave to cool in the poaching liquid.

To serve:
1. Place three halves of peaches onto six serving bowls. Add a scoop or two of the sorbet and scatter with the mint or lemon balm leaves. Serve.

The Essence - Contemporary recipes inspired by a traditional kitchen garden

# Roast peach with spiced brown bread and pistachio ice cream

Brown bread ice cream is one of my personal favourites. It is a combination of fresh custard (crème anglaise) and toasted sweetened brown breadcrumbs, with the addition of crushed pistachios in this recipe. It is not necessary to use an ice cream maker so there is no excuse for not preparing this dessert.
Serves 6

For the ice cream:
250g/ 9oz organic brown bread
250ml/ 9fl oz double cream
250ml/ 9fl oz milk
50g/ 2oz castor sugar
4 free-range organic egg yolks
75g/2 ½ oz demerara sugar
1 tsp ground mixed spice
50g/ 2oz peeled pistachios, crushed

For the peaches:
6 whole fresh peaches
50g/ 2oz unsalted butter
50g/ 2oz castor sugar
1 tsp vanilla essence
100ml/ 3 ½ fl oz white wine

To prepare the ice cream:
Pre-heat the grill to a medium-high temperature.
1. Using a food processor, blend the bread into fine breadcrumbs.
2. Mix the demerara sugar with the breadcrumbs and spread over a baking tray, then toast under the grill until they are all evenly golden brown.
3. Bring the cream and milk to the boil in a heavy based saucepan.
4. Meanwhile, whisk the egg yolks and sugar together until pale.
5. Pour in the cream and milk and return to the heat in a clean pan.
6. Stir over a low heat until thickened slightly and then remove and chill the saucepan over ice immediately.
7. Combine the breadcrumbs with the mixed spice and pistachios and then stir into the cream.
8. Transfer to a container and freeze until firm.

To prepare the peaches:
Pre-heat the oven to 200°C/ 400°F/ Gas mark 6.
1. Rinse, halve and stone the peaches.
2. In a large frying pan, heat the butter and then fry the peach halves until they have taken on a little colour. Add the sugar and caramelise lightly.
3. Add the wine and vanilla essence and transfer to the oven for 15 minutes.

To finish and serve:
1. Remove the peaches from the oven and divide between the serving plates. Spoon some of the cooking juices over the peaches.
2. Place a scoop or two of the ice cream next to the peaches and serve.

# Apricot bavarois set in a chilled apricot soup with garden blossoms

Chilled soup may sound a little unusual for a dessert, but here you have a really light, interesting and pretty dish that would be perfect for a lunchtime meal. You will need six small ramekins or Dariole moulds for this recipe.
Serves 6

For the bavarois:
500ml/ 18fl oz organic Soya milk
75g/ 2 ½oz castor sugar
1 tsp vanilla essence
5 fresh apricots
5 gelatine leaves, soaked in cold water until soft

For the chilled soup:
10 fresh apricots
250ml/ 9fl oz fresh orange juice
1 tbsp organic clear honey

Handful of mixed garden blossoms such as rose petals, nasturtium, Feoija flowers, Hemerocallis
Handful of tiny wild strawberries or raspberries

To prepare the bavarois:
1. Combine the milk, sugar and vanilla in a saucepan.
2. Rinse, stone and roughly chop the apricots and mix with the milk.
3. Bring to a simmer and cook gently for 10 minutes.
4. Stir in the gelatine until dissolved.
5. Transfer to a blender and puree until smooth.
6. Pass through a fine sieve and cool.
7. Pour into the six moulds and chill until set.

To prepare the chilled soup:
1. Rinse, stone and roughly chop the apricots.
2. Combine with orange juice and honey and puree until smooth.
3. Pass through a fine sieve and chill.

To finish and serve:
1. De-mould the bavarois, by briefly dipping each mould in hot water, and place in the centre of six chilled serving bowls.
2. Pour the chilled apricot soup around the bavarois.
3. Scatter the blossoms and berries in the soup and serve.

# Raspberry and Pimm's Jelly
# with cucumber and mint compote

This is a good alternative to the traditional Pimm's drink and would complement a summer barbeque perfectly.
Again, you will need six ramekins or jelly moulds for this dish.
Serves 6

For the jelly:
350g/ 12oz raspberries
100g/ 3 ½oz castor sugar
300ml/ 11fl oz lemonade
200ml/ 7fl oz Pimm's
6 gelatine leaves, soaked in cold water until soft

For the compote:
1 cucumber, peeled
1 orange
Handful small mint leaves

18 perfect raspberries for garnish

To prepare the jelly:
1.  Mix the raspberries with the sugar and Pimm's in a saucepan and bring to a simmer.
2.  Cook gently for 5 minutes and then stir in the gelatine.
3.  Chill until the mixture just starts to set, and then stir in the lemonade.
4.  Transfer to the moulds and leave to set in the fridge (approximately 1 ½ hours).

To prepare the compote:
1.  Cut the cucumber in 2cm/ ¾" dice.
2.  Grate the *zest* from the orange and then peel and segment it.
3.  Combine the cucumber with the zest, segments and mint leaves and leave to infuse for 10 minutes.

To finish and serve:
1.  De-mould the jelly, by briefly dipping each mould in a pan of hot water, and place onto six chilled serving plates and spoon some of the compote next to the jelly.
2.  Garnish with three of the perfect raspberries and serve.

# Raspberry soufflé with raspberry sauce and ginger ice cream

A perfect soufflé can be an indication of a great cook. The raspberries lend themselves well to a soufflé as their tartness cuts through the egg. The ginger provides a nice contrast to what should be a brilliant dinner party dessert. Be sure to practice this recipe at least once beforehand and double check the timings with your own oven. You will need six deep ramekins/soufflé dishes for this dessert as shown opposite.
Serves 6

For the soufflé base/pastry cream:
500ml/ 18fl oz milk
1 vanilla pod, split
6 organic free-range egg yolks
100g/ 3 ½oz castor sugar
25g/ 1oz cornflour
25g/ 1oz plain flour

For finishing the soufflé:
300g/ 10oz organic free-range egg whites
190g/ 6 ½oz castor sugar
30 raspberries

For preparation of the moulds:
50g/ 2oz unsalted butter
50g/ 2oz castor sugar

6 fresh mint leaves
Icing sugar for dusting

For the ginger ice cream:
250ml/ 9fl oz milk
250ml/ 9fl oz double cream
4 organic free-range egg yolks
100g/ 3 ½oz castor sugar
25g/ 1oz crystallised stem ginger

For the raspberry sauce:
450g/ 1lb fresh raspberries
Juice of 1 organic lemon
50g/ 2oz icing sugar

*Chefs tip*
*This recipe will make a little extra quantity than you will actually require. However, this works to your advantage meaning you do not have to scrape the last of the mix out of the bowl, thus knocking all the air out and having to serve a collapsed sixth soufflé.*

To prepare the soufflé base/pastry cream:
1. Bring the milk and vanilla pod to the boil in a heavy based saucepan.
2. Meanwhile, whisk the egg yolks and sugar together in a heatproof bowl until pale. Then whisk in the flour and cornflour.
3. Whisk the milk into the egg yolks and then return to the heat in a clean saucepan.
4. Bring to the boil and then continue to boil for 2-3 minutes, stirring constantly.
5. Pass through a fine sieve and then cool.

To prepare the ice cream:
1. Bring the milk and cream to the boil in a heavy based saucepan.
2. Meanwhile, whisk the egg yolks and sugar together in a heatproof bowl until pale.
3. Whisk the milk onto the egg yolks and return to the heat in a clean saucepan.
4. Cook gently until the mix thickens slightly.
5. Transfer to a bowl and cool over ice immediately.
6. Finely chop the ginger and add to the cream and then churn in an ice cream machine. Freeze.

To prepare the raspberry sauce:
1. Simply blend the raspberries with the icing sugar and lemon juice until smooth and then pass through a fine sieve. Reserve.

To prepare the ramekins:
1. Lightly grease the inside of the ramekins with butter and then make a 3mm/ ⅛″ rim of softened butter around the top inside edge of the ramekins. Dust the whole of the inside with castor sugar and then chill them in the fridge.

To cook and serve:
Pre-heat the oven to 190°C/ 375°F/ Gas mark 5.
1. Stir six tablespoons of the raspberry sauce into the soufflé base/pastry cream.
2. Place four raspberries into the base of each ramekin.
3. Using an electric whisk/mixer, lightly whisk the egg whites until voluminous.
4. Slowly add the castor sugar and continue to whisk until stiff and glossy.
5. Gently whisk a quarter of the egg white into the soufflé base and then gently fold in the rest using a metal spoon.
6. Spoon the mix into the ramekins and level the top with a palette knife.
7. Place in the centre of the oven and cook for about 11-14 minutes. This depends on the size of the ramekins and the heat distribution of the oven. The soufflés should be well risen and look firm but springy. Try not to open the oven door during the first 10 minutes of cooking.
8. Meanwhile, warm the raspberry sauce and scoop some ice cream into six side dishes.
9. Pour the raspberry sauce into a sauceboat and prepare the serving plates.
10. Once the soufflés are cooked, remove them quickly but carefully onto the serving plates and dust with icing sugar. Garnish with a raspberry, some mint and place the dish of ice cream onto the plate.
11. Serve and offer the warm raspberry sauce to your guests to pour into the soufflés.

# Rose petal scented macaroon
# with raspberry salad and coulis

Making macaroons requires a little more care and time during the preparation and cooking process. The results are spectacular with a crispy outside and slightly chewy middle. Here, this is combined with the tartness of fresh raspberries and some fragrant rose petals. I am grateful to the Roux Brothers for their basic macaroon recipe which can be found on pages 204-5 of their book, *The Roux Brothers on Patisserie, published by Little, Brown.*
Serves 6

For the macaroons:
225g/ 8oz icing sugar
125g/ 4oz ground almonds
4 organic free-range egg whites
25g/ 1oz castor sugar
1 tbsp chopped rose petals
A little red food colouring

100ml/ 3 ½fl oz double cream, whipped
Handful of mint leaves & small rose petals

For the salad and coulis:
750g/ 1lb 9oz fresh raspberries
50g/ 2oz icing sugar
Juice of 1 organic lemon

To prepare the macaroons:
1. Using a sieve, sift together the icing sugar and the almonds three times to mix evenly.
2. Whisk the egg whites until voluminous.
3. Add the sugar and continue to whisk until stiff.
4. Add the colouring and rose petals and whisk for 1 minute.
5. Sieve the almonds and icing sugar over the egg whites and fold them in until they are thoroughly blended and the mixture is smooth.
6. Line a baking tray with greaseproof paper.
7. Transfer the mix to a piping bag with a plain nozzle and pipe the mix into even rounds about 7cm/ 2 ¾" in diameter. You need two rounds per portion.
8. Leave the macaroons to rest for 20 minutes; meanwhile pre-heat the oven to 180°C/ 350°F/ Gas mark 4.
9. Bake the macaroons for 14 minutes with the oven door slightly ajar to allow the steam to escape.
10. Remove the macaroons from the oven and transfer the greaseproof paper onto a damp surface.
11. After 2-3 minutes remove from the greaseproof onto a clean tray and reserve.

To prepare the raspberry salad:
1. Take 250g/ 9oz of the raspberries and puree in a blender with the sugar and lemon juice until smooth. Pass through a fine sieve into a bowl and reserve.
2. Combine the raspberries with this coulis.

To finish and serve:
1. Join two macaroons together with a little whipped cream and then use a little cream to stick each macaroon to the centre of the serving plates.
2. Spoon some of the raspberry salad around the macaroon and scatter the rose petals and mint over the dish.

# Roasted figs served with vintage balsamic vinegar and ginger marscapone

Roasted figs have a wonderful taste, texture and aroma. Here, I have complemented the figs with some acidity from the vinegar and the spicy, creamy marscapone cheese.
Serves 6

For the roasted figs:
18 fresh figs
25g/ 1oz unsalted butter
50g/ 2oz demerara sugar
½ cinnamon stick
Splash of red wine

3 tbsp vintage balsamic vinegar

For the ginger marscapone:
200g/ 7oz low fat marscapone cheese
25g/ 1oz icing sugar
25g/ 1oz stem ginger in syrup, chopped
Grated *zest* of ½ organic lemon

To prepare the figs:
Pre-heat the oven to 200°C/ 400°F/ Gas mark 6.
1. Rinse the figs and remove any woody stalk.
2. Heat the butter in an oven-proof frying pan (no plastic handles), add the figs and lightly fry for 5 minutes.
3. Add the sugar and the cinnamon stick and lightly caramelise.
4. Add a splash of red wine to moisten and transfer the pan to the oven for 15 minutes.

To prepare the marscapone:
1. Combine the cheese, sugar, ginger and lemon zest together in a bowl.

To finish and serve:
1. Drizzle the balsamic vinegar onto six warmed serving plates.
2. Arrange the figs in a triangular pattern and spoon over any extra cooking juices.
3. Place a spoonful of marscapone between the figs and serve.

The Essence - Contemporary recipes inspired by a traditional kitchen garden

# Pistachio panna cotta with warm cherries and lavender

A fragrant Italian inspired dessert given extra texture by the addition of toasted pistachio nuts. There is a good contrast of colour here, and the dish has a delicious summery feel to it. You will need six wide but not too deep ramekins to set the panna cotta in.
Serves 6

For the panna cotta:
200ml/ 7fl oz milk
500ml/ 18fl oz double cream
1 vanilla pod, split
100g/ 3 ½oz icing sugar
100g/ 3 ½oz shelled pistachio nuts, crushed
4 gelatine leaves, soaked in cold water until soft

For the cherries:
450g/ 1lb cherries, halved & stoned
200ml/ 7fl oz fresh apple juice

1 tbsp crushed lavender petals
2 tbsp toasted shelled pistachio nuts

To prepare the panna cotta:
1. Combine the milk, double cream, icing sugar and vanilla pod in a saucepan and bring to the boil slowly.
2. Simmer for 2-3 minutes and then stir in the pistachio nuts and gelatine.
3. Remove from the heat and leave to *infuse* for 10 minutes.
4. Transfer to a blender and puree until smooth.
5. Pass through a muslin cloth or very fine sieve.
6. Pour into the moulds and chill in the fridge until set.

To prepare the cherries:
1. Combine the cherries with the apple juice in a saucepan and cook over a low heat until the cherries just begin to soften and 'bleed'. Remove from the heat and chill.

To finish and serve:
1. De-mould the panna cotta, by briefly dipping each mould in a pan of hot water, into six chilled shallow serving bowls.
2. Spoon the cherries around the panna cotta and sprinkle over the lavender petals and the pistachio nuts. Serve.

# Cherry compote with cinnamon,
# served with baked ricotta cheese and toasted almonds

Cherries are one of my favourite fruits; they are healthy, low in calories and very versatile. This is a warm dessert served with baked ricotta infused with fresh lemon zest. You could substitute almonds with brazil nuts, hazelnuts, macadamia nuts or pistachios if you so desire. You will need six 8cm/3″ diameter ovenproof ring moulds on a greaseproof lined baking tray.
Serves 6

For the cherry compote:
1 kg/ 2lb 2oz fresh cherries, stoned
100g/ 3 ½oz castor sugar
200ml/ 7fl oz fresh apple juice
2 cinnamon sticks

25g/ 1oz unsalted butter
100g/ 3 ½oz whole organic almonds, toasted

For the baked ricotta cheese:
300g/ 10oz organic ricotta cheese
50g/ 2oz icing sugar
Juice and zest of 1 organic lemon
2 free-range organic eggs

To prepare the baked ricotta cheese:
Pre-heat the oven to 190°C/ 375°F/ Gas mark 5.
1.  Grease the ring moulds with the unsalted butter.
2.  Combine the cheese, icing sugar, lemon and eggs together in a bowl and mix well.
3.  Spoon the mixture into the ring moulds and bake in the centre of the oven for approximately 15 minutes, until lightly golden brown, risen and springy to the touch.

Meanwhile, prepare the cherries:
1.  In a shallow saucepan, combine the cherries with sugar, apple juice and cinnamon.
2.  Cook over a medium to high heat, stirring regularly for about 10 minutes until the liquid has *reduced* to a glossy thick sauce.

To finish and serve:
1.  De-mould the baked ricotta, by running a thin knife around the inner circumference of the moulds, into six warmed serving bowls.
2.  Spoon the cherries around and sprinkle over the almonds. Serve.

# Plum feuilleté with fried cinnamon pastry cream and plum sauce

This is a dessert that needs a little more time in its preparation. As suggested for the rhubarb and Blood orange tart on page 82, you can either use good quality ready made puff pastry or you can make your own from the recipe on page 268. I love the combination of textures in this dish as you cut through the crisp, flaky pastry and into the soft, rich pastry cream.
Serves 6

For the pastry cream:
1lt/ 1 ¾ pints organic whole milk
6 free-range organic egg yolks
200g/ 7oz castor sugar
100g/ 3 ½oz cornflour
1 tsp vanilla extract
1 tsp ground cinnamon

For the plum *feuilleté*:
450g/ 1 lb fresh puff pastry (see basics)
100g/ 3 ½oz icing sugar
6-10 ripe plums, washed & stoned

For the plum sauce:
6 ripe plums, washed & stoned
350ml/ 12fl oz apple juice
75g/ 2 ½oz castor sugar

To finish the dish:
50g/ 2oz unsalted butter
6 sprigs of mint
Icing sugar for dusting

To prepare the pastry cream:
1. Line a 25x20x2cm/ 10x8x ¾″ baking tray with Clingfilm.
2. Bring the milk, vanilla and cinnamon to the boil in a heavy based saucepan.
3. Meanwhile, whisk together the egg yolks, cornflour and sugar until pale and ribbon-like.
4. Slowly pour the milk onto the eggs, mixing well.
5. Return to the heat in a clean pan. Bring back to the boil and cook for 3-4minutes, stirring constantly. You should no longer be able to taste the cornflour.
6. Pass through a sieve, pour onto the baking tray, level and chill.

To prepare the feuilleté:
Pre-heat the oven to 220°C/ 425°F/ Gas mark 7.
1. On a lightly floured surface, roll out the pastry to an even thickness of 5mm/ ¼″. Transfer to a lightly greased or lined large baking tray and chill.
2. Cover the pastry with a layer of greaseproof paper and top with another baking tray. Weigh down evenly with heatproof weights.
3. Bake at the top of the oven for approximately 20-25 minutes until the pastry is crisp and lightly golden.
4. Dust the pastry with the icing sugar and return to the oven to gently caramelise the sugar.
5. Remove the pastry and carefully cut into eighteen even sized squares or rectangles.

To prepare the plum sauce:
1. Simmer the plums, apple juice and sugar together until the quantity has reduced by half.
2. Puree in a blender and pass through a fine sieve. Keep warm.

To finish and serve:
1. Slice each of the fresh plums into thin slices.
2. Cut the pastry cream into eighteen even sized pieces, the same shape as your pastry, but a little smaller in overall size.
3. Divide the butter between two large frying pans and fry the pastry cream squares until lightly golden on each side.
4. On six warmed serving plates, make a pool of the plum sauce.
5. Place a piece of pastry onto the sauce and then top with the pastry cream and some plum slices.
6. Repeat this and finish with a piece of caramelised pastry.
7. Dust with icing sugar, garnish with mint and serve.

# Preserving

Jam making is an obvious way of preserving and storing summer and autumn fruits. The jam is sterilised by intense boiling. The jam jars you use will need to be sterilised before use. Sterilising solutions are commonly available at chemists.

You will require the following equipment for jam making:

Scales
A large preserving pan
Long handled wooden spoons
Sugar thermometer
Stainless steel jug with pouring lip
Jam jars and lids
Waxed jam covers
Decorative lids

# Victoria plum and lavender jam

Makes about 1 ½ kg/ 3lbs:

2kg/ 4 ¼lbs just ripe Victoria plums
2kg/ 4 ¼lbs preserving sugar
2 tbsp crushed lavender petals

1.  Halve and stone the plums. Combine the plums with the sugar and leave to stand overnight in a plastic container.
2.  Transfer the plums and sugar to a large preserving pan and heat gently until the sugar has dissolved.
3.  Increase the heat and boil quickly until the jam reaches setting point. *Skim* off any impurities that rise to the surface during this period. This occurs around 105°C/ 212°F. You can also test the setting point by spooning a little jam onto a chilled plate and checking if the jam sets.
4.  Remove from the heat, add the lavender petals and pour into warm dry jars.
5.  Cover with a waxed jam cover, place a lid on the jar, label and store the jam in a cool, dark place.

# Raspberry and ginger-rosemary jam

Raspberries come thick and fast from late July through to late September in the right conditions. I always aim to make use of as many raspberries as possible, whether it's through simply freezing them for use in desserts, or making sorbet, vinegar, purees, jam or bottled raspberries. Here, I have combined them with ginger scented rosemary. These are two flavours that have a wonderful affinity for each other and complement the raspberries particularly well. If you don't have any ginger-rosemary, then simply use normal rosemary and add some finely grated root ginger.

Makes about 1 ½ kg/ 3lbs:

2kg/ 4 ¼lbs fresh raspberries
2kg/ 4 ¼lbs preserving sugar
2 tbsp finely chopped ginger-rosemary

1.  Combine the raspberries and sugar together and leave in a plastic bowl overnight.
2.  Put the raspberries and sugar into a preserving pan and bring to the boil slowly.
3.  Increase the heat and boil rapidly until setting point is achieved. *Skim* off any impurities that may rise to the surface during this period. This will occur around 105°C/ 212°F. You can also test for setting point by spooning a little jam onto a chilled plate and checking if the jam sets.
4.  Once setting point is reached, add the ginger-rosemary and remove the pan from the heat. Pour the jam into clean, warm jars. Cover with a waxed jam cover; place a lid on the jar, label, and store in a cool, dark place.

# Redcurrant jelly

I love making redcurrant jelly because I really appreciate how well it can flavour sauces to accompany red meat and game, as well as being the perfect condiment to roast lamb, chicken and raised pork and game pies.

Redcurrants, washed
900g/ 2lbs preserving sugar to every 1.2lts/ 2 pints of juice extracted (see below)

1.  Pre-heat the oven to 170°C/ 325°F/ Gas mark 3.
2.  Place the redcurrants in a large casserole, cover and place in the oven for 1 – 1 ½ hours.
3.  Remove from the oven and mash the fruit with a potato masher.
4.  Transfer the redcurrants to a muslin or jelly bag and drain into a plastic bowl overnight.
5.  Measure the extracted juice into a preserving pan and add the required amount of sugar.
6.  Bring to the boil slowly and then increase the heat and boil rapidly until setting point is reached. *Skim* off any impurities that may rise to the surface during this period. Setting point occurs around 105°C/ 212°F. You can also test for setting point by spooning a little of the jelly onto a chilled plate and checking if it sets.
7.  Once the jelly is ready, remove from the heat and pour into warm, dry jars.
8.  Place a lid on the jars, label and store in a cool, dark place.

# Tomato and chilli chutney

I find this an excellent way to use up any extra tomatoes. This chutney intensifies and enriches in flavour over time, and is the sort of preserve that I prepare a season in advance. You can use any type of tomatoes in this recipe; in fact, I think a variety of tomatoes provides an excellent result in taste, colour and texture.

Makes about 2 ½ kg/ 5lbs:

2kg/ 4 ¼ lbs tomatoes of your choice
3 large onions, peeled & chopped into 1cm dice
6 cloves of garlic, peeled & crushed
100g/ 3 ½oz organic golden sultanas
2-4 long red fresh chillies, finely sliced
1 tsp allspice
2 tsp coriander seeds
1 tsp fennel seeds
2 tsp thyme leaves
1lt/ 1 ¾ pints white wine vinegar
350g/ 12 oz preserving sugar
Sea salt & black pepper

1. Place all the ingredients except the sugar into a large preserving/jam pan and simmer for 1 hour until most of the liquid has been driven off.
2. Stir in the sugar and cook gently until the sugar has dissolved.
3. Increase the heat and boil rapidly, stirring, until the chutney is thick.
4. Season the chutney and pour into warm, dry jars. Cover with a lid, label, and store in a cool, dark place.

# Pickled baby vegetables and baby onions

As the autumn approaches, I love to enjoy lunches of homemade pâté, raised pork and game pies and sliced glazed ham. As an accompaniment I like these pickled baby vegetables that provide a good contrast in taste and texture.

For the pickling vinegar:
2lts/ 2 ½ pints malt vinegar
1 tsp coriander seeds
1 tsp black peppercorns
1 tsp allspice berries
6 cloves
1 star anise
1 long red chilli, split
1 tsp mustard seeds
2 garlic cloves, peeled & finely crushed

For the vegetables: (1 ½ kg in total)
Baby carrots, rinsed & scraped
Baby cauliflower florets
Young leeks, washed & trimmed
Baby turnips, washed
Baby sweet corn, washed
Baby courgettes, washed & sliced
Baby onions, peeled & trimmed

1. Place all the pickling ingredients in a stainless steel saucepan.
2. Bring to a simmer and then remove from the heat. Leave to stand for 2 -3 hours and then strain through a fine sieve or muslin cloth. Cool.
3. *Blanch* the baby vegetables in boiling salted water. *Refresh* in iced water, drain and pat dry.
4. Arrange the vegetables attractively in tall preserving jars.
5. Pour the cold vinegar over the vegetables, seal with a lid, label and store for up to six months in a cool, dark place.

Honey making

# Autumn

As seen in recent years, an "Indian summer" can seem to lead into what is traditionally thought of as autumn. September provides a bounty of quality and plentiful produce. As we move into October and November, we look forward to a full range of apples, pears, potatoes and leafy greens as well as the old English country garden fruits such as Quince and Medlar fruit.

Autumn is the perfect time to be making chutney and this provides an opportunity for you to stretch your imagination and repertoire with different flavour combinations. Autumn is also a time when the storage of fruits, potatoes and onions can provide for those forthcoming winter months.

In this chapter, you will find recipes for the aforementioned foods as well as pumpkin, butternut squash, cauliflower, crosnes, carrots, celery, cèpes, corn and onions.

# Purple potato crisps with truffle mayonnaise

The simplicity of this dish belies the sensational combination of the humble potato and the rare luxurious truffle. You can grow purple potatoes (also known as blue or truffle potatoes) in your garden as an alternative to normal varieties. I have also found them at local farm shops and farmers' markets. They make excellent roast potatoes, crisp fluffy chips and an unusual colourful mashed potato.
Serves 6

12 even sized large purple potatoes
1 lt/ 1 ¾pints vegetable oil

For the truffle mayonnaise:
2 free-range organic egg yolks
½ tsp Dijon mustard
150ml/ 5fl oz white wine vinegar
4 black peppercorns
½ bayleaf
250ml/ 9fl oz groundnut oil
Juice of ½ organic lemon
1 tsp white truffle oil
1 whole truffle, cleaned & finely chopped
Sea salt & white pepper

Preparation:
1. Peel and cut the potatoes into 2mm thick slices. Wash the slices very well in cold water and then soak them in cold water for 2 hours. Drain and wash the slices again, then drain and dry them on kitchen paper.
2. Meanwhile, in a small saucepan, *reduce* the vinegar, peppercorns and bayleaf by half. Pass through a fine sieve and cool.
3. Whisk the egg yolks with the vinegar and mustard in a bowl until pale.
4. Gradually whisk in the groundnut oil until it has completely emulsified.
5. Season with salt, pepper and lemon juice.
6. Stir in the truffle and truffle oil.

To cook the potatoes:
1. Heat the oil to 180°C/ 350°F in a deep saucepan or deep fat fryer.
2. Fry the potatoes in small batches until they are crisp and lightly golden.
3. Drain the crisps on kitchen paper and then season.
4. Serve with the truffle mayonnaise on the side.

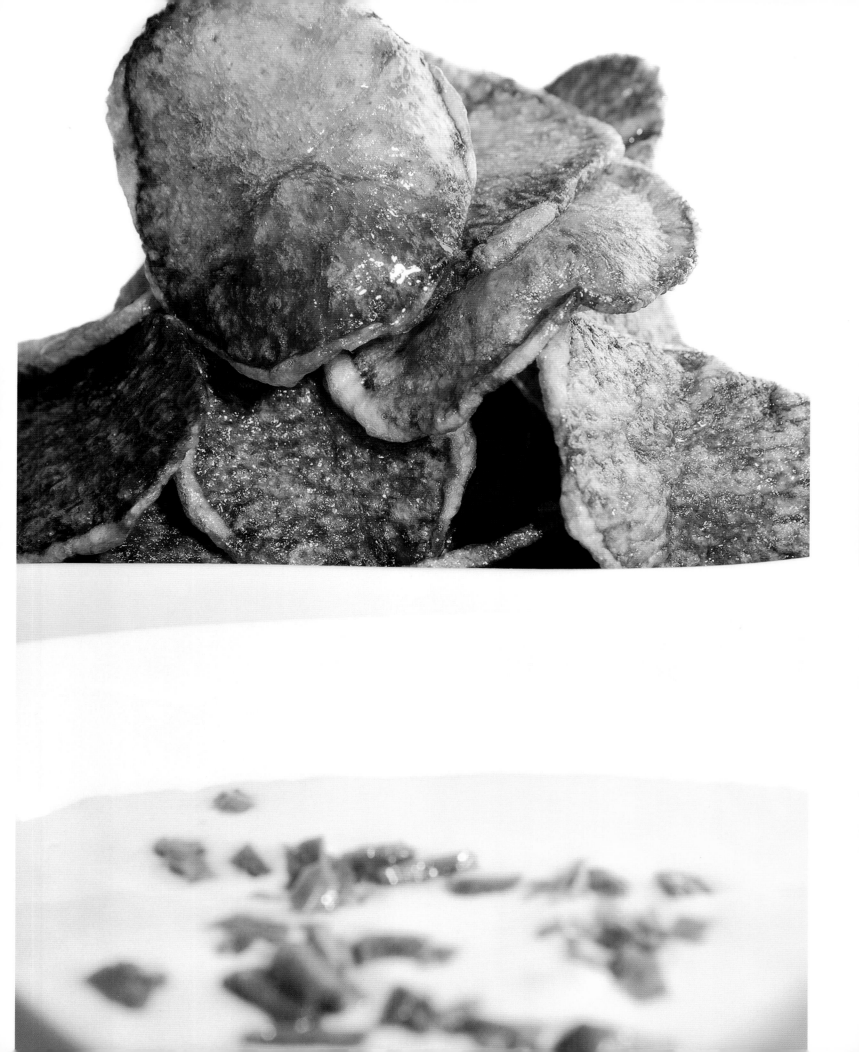

# Butternut squash custard flan
# with apple-walnut dressing and crispy onions

The butternut squash creates a smooth, velvety custard which combines well with the sweetness of the apple and the crispy onions. I find it useful to keep some pastry lined flan cases in the freezer which are perfect for preparing this style of dish at short notice. Individual 12cm x 2cm/ 4 ½" x ¾" deep flan cases are required here; these are available at many cookware shops.
Serves 6

For the flan cases:
200g/ 7oz plain organic flour
75g/ 2 ½ oz unsalted butter
25g/ 1oz finely grated Parmigiano Regiano cheese
1 tbsp toasted pine nuts, finely crushed
1 tsp toasted sesame seeds
1 free-range egg yolk
Cold water

For the butternut squash custard:
200g/ 7oz butternut squash flesh
2 free-range organic eggs
250ml/ 8 fl oz whole organic milk
A pinch of ground coriander
A pinch of grated nutmeg
A pinch of ground cumin

For the apple-walnut dressing:
4 Cox's or Granny Smith apples
75g/ 2 ½oz toasted walnut pieces
25ml/ 1 fl oz sherry vinegar
100ml/ 3 ½ fl oz extra virgin olive oil
1 tbsp flat-leaf parsley, roughly chopped

For the garnish:
2 white onions
100ml/ 3 ½ fl oz whole organic milk
100g/ 3 ½oz plain organic flour

Sea salt & black pepper
Melted butter & flour for lining the flan cases.
Vegetable oil for deep frying

To prepare the pastry and flan cases:
1. Season the flour and sift into a bowl. Dice the butter and rub into the flour until the mixture resembles fine breadcrumbs.
2. Stir in the pine nuts, cheese and sesame seeds.
3. Mix in the egg yolk, bring together and slowly add enough cold water to form a smooth dough. Wrap in Clingfilm and rest in the fridge for at least 30 minutes.
4. Pre-heat the oven to 190°C/ 375°F/ Gas mark 5.
5. Grease and flour six individual flan cases.
6. Roll out the pastry to an even thickness of about 3mm/ ⅛".
7. Cut out circles a few centimetres larger than the flan cases. Line the cases with the pastry, pressing the pastry firmly but carefully into the edges. Leave an overhang of about 1cm/ ½" that can be trimmed at a later stage. Chill the cases for 20 minutes.
8. Pour some baking beans into the flan cases and *'blind bake'* in the oven until lightly golden brown and the pastry is cooked throughout.
9. Remove the cases, remove the beans and reserve.

To prepare the butternut squash custard:
1. Steam or boil the butternut squash until tender, and then puree in a food blender until very smooth.
2. Cool and reserve.
3. Whisk the eggs and milk together and mix in the cooled squash puree.
4. Add the coriander, nutmeg and cumin and then season. Pass through a fine sieve and reserve.

To cook the squash flans:
Pre-heat the oven to 180°C/ 350°F/ Gas mark 4.
1. Pour the butternut custard into the flan cases and bake in the oven for approximately 20-25 minutes, until the custard has just set and is lightly coloured.
2. Remove the flans from the oven, cool and then remove the pastry from the flan case. Trim the edges of the pastry with some scissors. Reserve.

To prepare the apple-walnut dressing:
1. Peel, core and dice the apples into 1cm/ ½″ cubes.
2. Combine with the walnuts, oil, vinegar and parsley and season to taste.

To prepare the crispy onions:
1. Heat the oil to 190°C/ 375°F in a deep saucepan or a deep fat fryer.
2. Peel and slice the onions thinly to produce thin whole rounds of onion.
3. Pass the onions through the milk and then the flour and fry in the oil until crispy.
4. Drain on kitchen paper before serving.

To finish and serve:
1. Re-heat the flans in the oven and place them in the centre of six warmed serving plates.
2. Garnish with the apple-walnut dressing and top with the onion rings. Serve.

# Roasted pumpkin salad with organic feta cheese and pickled walnuts

This dish is adorned with colourful ingredients and different textures which would serve as a great lunch dish as well as an autumnal starter.
Serves 6

1 pumpkin weighing about 2kg/ 4 ¼ lb (yielding about 1.2kg/ 2 ½ lb of flesh)
3 tbsp groundnut oil
1 garlic clove, peeled & finely crushed
½ tsp coriander seeds
¼ tsp cumin seeds
¼ tsp fennel seeds
300g/ 10oz organic feta cheese, cubed
100g/ 3 ½oz pickled walnuts, sliced
1 tbsp snipped chives
1 tbsp flat parsley leaves, roughly chopped
3 slices organic wholegrain bread, cubed
Extra virgin olive oil
Sea salt & black pepper

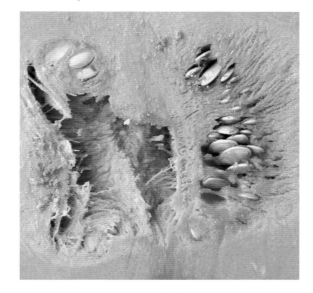

Pre-heat the oven to 200°C/ 400°F/ Gas mark 6.
1. Peel and halve the pumpkin. Scoop out the seeds with a melon baller and cut the flesh into even chunky slices. Twenty four to thirty slices would be ideal.
2. Combine the pumpkin with the groundnut oil, garlic and spices in a bowl and season well. Leave to *infuse* for 30 minutes.
3. Heat 1 tbsp of the oil in a large oven-proof frying pan (no plastic handles) and fry the pumpkin on all sides, until it is coloured nicely. You may need to do this in two stages.
4. Place the pumpkin into the oven and cook for 15 minutes, until the flesh has softened but not lost its texture.
5. Remove the pumpkin and arrange the slices equally on six warmed serving plates. Garnish with the feta cheese and walnuts.
6. In the same frying pan, heat the remaining 2 tbsp of the oil and quickly fry the cubed bread until crispy. Season and sprinkle over the pumpkin.
7. Finish with the snipped chives and flat parsley and drizzle with olive oil. Serve.

# Sauté of cèpes and prawns with spinach, sweet and sour vinaigrette

Cèpes come into season during September, and are particularly good sautéed. Their texture complements this method of cooking and they caramelise beautifully. If you can't find these particular ingredients you could substitute the cèpes with organic chestnut mushrooms and the prawns with lobster. Cèpes do vary in quality somewhat. I prefer to use medium sized mushrooms about 5-10cm/ 2-4″ in length. I also prefer to use ones that don't have too much yellow foamy flesh under the cap. Cèpes can also become infested with maggots, so I always first slice open at least one from the batch I'm about to purchase.
Serves 6

For the principal ingredients:
350g/ 12oz fresh cèpes
18 large prawn tails, shelled
75g/ 2 ½oz spinach leaves, washed
2 green apples
2 tbsp flaked almonds, toasted
4 tbsp olive oil
½ garlic clove, peeled & finely crushed
Sea salt & black pepper

For the vinaigrette:
Juice of 1 organic orange
Juice of 1 grapefruit
100ml/ 3 ½ fl oz tomato juice
1 tbsp soft brown sugar
50ml/ 2 fl oz red wine vinegar
50ml/ 2 fl oz olive oil
1 tsp wholegrain mustard

To prepare the vinaigrette:
1. Combine the juices, sugar and vinegar in a small saucepan and *reduce* by a quarter over a medium heat. Cool, and then whisk in the olive oil and mustard then season to taste.

To prepare the principle ingredients:
1. Scrub the cèpes with a soft nail brush to remove any soil. Rinse lightly and then slice the cèpes in half.
2. Remove the intestinal tract from the prawns.
3. Thoroughly wash the spinach, remove the stalks and dry well in a salad spinner.
4. Core the apples and cut into *julienne*.
5. Heat half of the oil in a large frying pan and *sauté* the cèpes until lightly golden. Season and reserve.
6. Using the same pan, sauté the prawns in 1 tbsp of the oil for 3-4 minutes until cooked through. Season and reserve.
7. Add the final tbsp of oil to the frying pan, and add the spinach and garlic and cook for a minute or so until the spinach has wilted slightly.

To finish and serve:
1. On six warmed serving plates, equally arrange the cèpes, prawns and spinach.
2. Dress with the vinaigrette, sprinkle with the apple julienne and almonds and serve.

# Pan-fried scallops with white onion puree, leeks and coriander vinaigrette

Scallops are at their best during the autumn and colder months. I only use hand-dived caught scallops; dredging scallops causes damage to the sea bed and coral. As with all fish (and especially shellfish) take your time to search out the best supplier in your local area. Hand-dived scallops are more expensive, but the results speak for themselves in both the cooking process and eating. As for the scallop roe (the bright orange part), I prefer to remove it from the scallop first but this is due to personal preference.
Serves 6

For the white onion puree:
3 large white onions, peeled
1 garlic clove, peeled
3 cloves
1 bayleaf
500ml/ 18 fl oz organic milk
500ml/ 18 fl oz vegetable stock (see basics)

For the coriander vinaigrette:
100ml/ 3 ½ fl oz extra virgin olive oil
25ml/ 1 fl oz white wine vinegar
½ tsp English mustard
Juice of ½ organic lemon
2 tbsp chopped coriander leaves

18 large fresh hand-dived scallops
2 leeks, washed & sliced into 1 cm/ ½" rounds
1 tbsp groundnut oil
Salt & black pepper

To prepare the onion puree:
1.  Stud the onions with the cloves and cover with the milk in a deep saucepan with the bayleaf and garlic.
2.  Bring to a simmer and cook until the onions are completely soft. Remove from the milk and discard the cloves.
3.  Blend the onions in a food processor until very smooth. You may need to add a little milk to aid the blending. The result should be a thick, smooth, velvety puree. Season to taste and reserve.

To prepare the coriander vinaigrette:
1.  Combine the ingredients in a bowl and season to taste.

To prepare the scallops (Fig.1):
1.  Open the scallop shells and carefully slice down the flat half of the shell to expose the scallop (Fig.2). Carefully scoop out the scallop with a spoon. Remove the outer skirt and coral if desired (Fig.3).
2.  Rinse the scallop quickly and pat dry on kitchen paper (Fig.4).
3.  Chill until required.

To finish and serve:

1. Re-heat the onion puree in a saucepan.
2. Steam the leeks until just tender. Season and reserve.
3. Heat a large non-stick frying pan and add the oil. Add the scallops and fry for 30 seconds on each side. You may need to do this in two batches in order not to overload the pan and lose the heat. Remove the scallops from the pan onto six warmed serving plates.
4. Arrange a few slices of leeks around the scallops and place some teaspoonfuls of the puree around the plate.
5. Dress with the coriander vinaigrette and serve.

Pan-fried scallops with white onion puree, leeks and coriander vinaigrette

# Free-range organic chicken pancakes
## with celery and lemon salad

I really love this starter. The delicate pancake opens to reveal tender, flavourful chicken. The acidulated celery salad gives the dish texture and a citrus kick. Deep-fried celery leaves provide a crispy finish.
Serves 6

For the pancake batter:
400ml/ 14fl oz whole organic milk
100g/ 3 ½ oz strong organic flour
2 free-range organic eggs
1 tsp thyme leaves
Grated *zest* of ½ organic lemon

For the celery salad:
6 sticks celery
Juice of ½ organic lemon
2 tbsp extra virgin olive oil
1 tbsp snipped chives

For the chicken filling:
4 free-range organic chicken breasts
3 sticks celery
2 green apples
3 tbsp mayonnaise
Juice of ½ organic lemon

Handful of celery leaves
500ml/ 18fl oz vegetable oil
500ml/ 18fl oz chicken stock (see basics)
Selection of herbs to garnish
Extra virgin olive oil to garnish
Salt & black pepper

For the chicken filling:
1. Trim the chicken breasts of any skin, fat or sinew.
2. Place in a saucepan and cover with the chicken stock. Bring to a simmer and *poach* for 10 minutes. Leave to cool in the stock.
3. Cut the chicken into rough 2cm/ ¾ ″ cubes.
4. Wash and thinly slice the celery then combine with the chicken in a bowl.
5. Wash, quarter, core and cut the apple into *julienne*. Add to the chicken with the lemon juice and mayonnaise. Mix together. Season to taste and reserve.

For the pancakes:
1. Whisk together the milk, flour and eggs. Season and rest for 20 minutes. Pass through a fine sieve and mix in the thyme and lemon zest.
2. In a large non-stick frying or pancake pan, heat a little oil.
3. Add enough pancake batter to cover the base very thinly. Cook over a medium heat until the underside is sealed and lightly coloured. Flip the pancake and repeat. Remove and reserve. Repeat to make six pancakes.

For the celery:
1. Wash, peel and cut the celery into julienne. Combine with the olive oil, lemon juice and chives. Season to taste.

For the crispy celery leaves:
1. Heat the oil to 180°C/ 350°F in a deep saucepan or deep fat fryer. Add the celery leaves in small batches and fry until crispy and golden. Remove and drain on kitchen paper.

To finish and serve:
1. Lay the pancakes out on a work surface and divide the chicken filling into the centre of each pancake.
2. Fold the pancakes in and over to form a neat square parcel.
3. Place the pancakes in the centre of six serving plates and arrange some celery salad around each one.
4. Sprinkle with the herb selection, the crispy celery leaves and a little olive oil then serve.

# Creamy cauliflower soup with crosnes and mustard oil

Crosnes, also known as Chinese artichokes, are becoming more popular and abundant despite their slightly odd appearance. They are excellent sautéed with a little olive oil, seasoning and lemon juice. For this recipe I have also added some sautéed grated cauliflower and mustard oil which gives a little heat and really brings the soup to life.

Serves 6

750g/ 1lb 11oz cauliflower florets, washed
1 large onion, peeled & finely chopped
1 garlic clove, peeled & finely crushed
2 sticks celery, washed & thinly sliced
3 tbsp vegetable oil
200ml/ 7fl oz dry white wine
1lt/ 1 ¾ pints vegetable stock (see basics)
1 bouquet garni (see basics)
3 tbsp crème fraîche

200g/ 7oz crosnes, washed & trimmed
1 tbsp olive oil
Squeeze of organic lemon juice

Mustard oil to garnish (see basics)
1 tbsp snipped chives

Sea salt & black pepper

To prepare the soup:
1. Heat the oil in a large saucepan and gently sweat the onion, garlic and celery until softened.
2. Reserving a few florets, add the cauliflower and cook for a further 5 minutes.
3. Add the white wine, increase the heat and *reduce* by half. Pour in the stock and add the bouquet garni. Bring to the boil and simmer for 20-25 minutes until the cauliflower is soft.
4. Transfer to a blender and puree until smooth. Pour back into the pan and stir in the crème fraîche. Season to taste and keep warm.

To finish and serve:
1. Grate the remaining few florets finely.
2. Heat the spoonful of olive oil in a frying pan and *sauté* the crosnes and grated cauliflower until lightly coloured. Season and add the lemon juice.
3. Re-heat the soup and pour into six warmed serving bowls. Sprinkle the crosnes and cauliflower onto the soup and drizzle with mustard oil. Sprinkle with chives and serve.

# Red snapper and coriander fishcakes
# with spiced carrot salad, peanut-soy dressing

Very delicate, light fishcakes are the basis to this Oriental inspired dish. You could use wild sea bass, wild sea bream or swordfish instead of the snapper. This is a good chance to use some of that fresh coriander you've been growing.
Serves 6

For the fishcakes:
1 kg/ 2lb 2oz red snapper fillet, skinless & boneless
2 tbsp coriander, finely chopped
2 free-range organic egg whites
Grated zest & juice of 1 lime

For the peanut-soy dressing:
100g/ 3 ½oz unsalted peanuts
4 tbsp light soy sauce
½ tsp ground ginger
4 tbsp groundnut oil

For the spiced carrot salad:
450g/ 1lb carrots, peeled & trimmed
1 long red chilli, de-seeded
1 tbsp toasted sesame oil
1 tbsp rice wine vinegar

450g/ 1lb *Panko* breadcrumbs
6 tbsp groundnut oil
50g/ 2oz unsalted butter
Coriander to garnish
Sea salt & black pepper

To prepare the fishcakes:
1. Using a large, sharp knife and a large secure chopping board, mince the fish finely. The result should be homogeneous but not a puree.
2. Combine with the coriander, egg white and lime in a bowl and season.
3. Test for seasoning by frying a teaspoonful. Adjust if required.
4. Form the mix into twelve even sized rounds and chill for 1 hour.

To prepare the peanut-soy dressing:
1. Heat a large frying pan and dry roast the peanuts until lightly coloured.
2. Combine the peanuts with the soy sauce, ginger and oil. Reserve.

To prepare the spiced carrot salad:
1. Using a vegetable peeler, peel the carrot into fine, long ribbons.
2. *Blanch* in a pan of boiling salted water for 20 seconds. *Refresh* in iced water and drain.
3. Slice the chilli very thinly.
4. Combine the carrot ribbons with the chilli, sesame oil and vinegar in a bowl then season.

To finish and serve:
1. Coat the fishcakes in the breadcrumbs, ensuring you have a nice even coating.
2. Heat half the groundnut oil in a large frying pan and *sauté* six fishcakes on each side until golden. Add half the butter and glaze the fishcakes.
3. Remove the fishcakes and keep warm in a low oven and then repeat to cook the remaining six. On six warmed serving plates, arrange some carrot salad, two fishcakes and then spoon some dressing around. Sprinkle over the coriander and serve.

Red snapper and
coriander fishcakes with spiced carrot
salad, peanut-soy dressing

Fillets of brill glazed with mustard and tarragon mayonnaise, served with pink fir apple potatoes and a red onion dressing

# Fillets of Brill glazed with mustard and tarragon mayonnaise, served with Pink Fir Apple potatoes and a red onion dressing

Depending on the weather conditions and planting schedules, this is the time of year when those lovely Pink Fir Apple potatoes are lifted; they have a pinkish tinge, uneven texture and nutty flavour. If you can't manage to find Brill, you could use young wild halibut, turbot or thick plaice fillets. You will have extra mayonnaise but it will keep for up to week in the fridge.
Serves 6

For the Brill and mayonnaise:
1kg/ 2lb 2oz Brill fillet, skinned & divided into six
3 free-range organic egg yolks
25ml/ 1fl oz tarragon vinegar
175ml/ 6fl oz olive oil
2 tsp wholegrain mustard
2 tsp tarragon leaves, finely chopped

6 portions green vegetables of your choice
2tbsp herb oil (see basics)
Sea salt & black pepper

For the dressing:
25ml/ 1fl oz red wine vinegar
1 large red onion, finely chopped
Juice of ½ organic lemon
100ml/ 3 ½fl oz extra virgin olive oil
1 tbsp snipped chives
1 tbsp flat parsley leaves, chopped

450g/ 1lb Pink Fir Apple potatoes
Tarragon & chervil to garnish

To prepare the Brill and mayonnaise:
1. Whisk two of the egg yolks and the vinegar together. Drizzle in the oil, whisking constantly. Mix in the mustard, tarragon and season. Whisk in the final egg yolk.
2. Lay the Brill fillets onto a non-stick baking tray and spread the mayonnaise over the fish. Chill until required.

To prepare the dressing:
1. Mix the vinegar, red onion and lemon juice together. Season and slowly whisk in the olive oil. Stir in the chives and parsley.

To prepare the potatoes and vegetables:
1. Wash and lightly scrub the potatoes. Place in a large saucepan and cover with water. Season, bring to the boil and simmer until tender. Drain, and slice into neat 5mm/ ¼" thick circles. Reserve.
2. Prepare and cook the vegetables to your liking.

To finish and serve:
1. Pre-heat the grill to a medium heat. Cook the Brill under the grill until the fish is cooked through and the mayonnaise nicely glazed (about 4 minutes).
2. Meanwhile, reheat the potatoes and vegetables and dress with the herb oil.
3. Arrange on six warmed serving plates as shown in the photograph. Serve.

# Butter roasted partridge with creamed honeyed corn, sautéed greens and fig vinaigrette

The Partridge season begins during September. The most common breed to be found in Britain is the grey-legged partridge, although occasionally the red-legged variety makes an appearance. Fresh corn is an ingredient that is traditionally associated with the transition between summer and autumn and it combines beautifully with the outgoing figs and incoming greens such as the cabbage varieties and curly kale. Oven-ready partridge are readily available and are recommended unless you are a dab hand at preparing game.
Serves 6

**For the partridge:**
6 fresh oven ready partridge
6 rashers streaky bacon
3 bay leaves
6 sprigs thyme
6 sprigs rosemary
12 juniper berries
100g/ 3 ½ oz unsalted butter

**For the creamed honeyed corn:**
3 fresh corn-on-the-cob, sheath removed
6 tbsp groundnut oil
25g/ 1oz unsalted butter
1 garlic clove, peeled & finely crushed
250ml/ 9fl oz double cream
2 tbsp clear wild flower honey

**For the fig vinaigrette:**
6 ripe figs
½ garlic clove, peeled & finely crushed
25ml/ 1fl oz red wine vinegar
100ml/ 3 ½ fl oz extra virgin olive oil

**For the sautéed greens:**
300g/ 10oz mixed greens, cabbage & curly kale
1 tbsp groundnut oil

Sea salt & black pepper

To prepare the creamed honeyed corn:
Pre-heat the oven to 200°C/400°F/Gas mark 6
1. Brush the corn with the groundnut oil and season well.
2. Wrap each corn in tin foil and place on a baking tray in the oven.
3. Cook for 1 hour or until the corn is tender and the kernels come away from the cob easily. Cut the corn kernels away from the cob and mix in a bowl with a fork to break up the kernels.
4. Heat the butter in a non-stick frying pan and gently fry the garlic for 30 seconds. Add the corn kernels and honey and *sauté* for 1 minute. Finish with the cream and *reduce* the liquid quantity by half. Season and reserve.

Meanwhile, prepare the fig vinaigrette:
1.  Remove the small stalk and a little of the base from the fig and then chop them into rough 5mm/ ¼″ dice. Whisk the garlic, vinegar and olive oil together in a bowl and add the figs. Season and reserve.

To prepare the greens:
1.  Rinse the greens well and remove any particularly woody stalks. Break into bite-sized pieces.
2.  Bring a large saucepan of salted water to the boil and *blanch* the greens for 2 minutes.
3.  Drain the greens and immediately plunge into iced water to *refresh* them. Drain again, pat dry and reserve.

To cook the partridge:
Pre-heat the oven to 220°C/425°F/Gas mark 7
1.  Place half a bayleaf, a sprig of thyme and rosemary and two juniper berries into the cavity of each partridge. Season well and place a rasher of bacon around each bird.
2.  Heat the butter in a large frying pan and fry the partridge on all sides until lightly browned all over.
3.  Transfer the birds to a roasting tray, spoon the cooking butter and juices over them and place the tray in the oven. Reserve the frying pan you have cooked the partridge in.
4.  Cook the partridge for 10-12 minutes until they feel firm to the touch. You can also test them by piercing the meat with a skewer to see if the juices run clear. Try not to overcook the partridge otherwise the meat will be dry. Once cooked, remove from the oven and *rest* the birds upside down for 5 minutes. This will enable the juices to run back into the breast meat.

To finish and serve:
1.  Whilst the partridge are cooking, heat 1 tbsp of groundnut oil in the same frying pan you cooked the partridge in and sauté the greens for 3 minutes. This will enhance the taste of the greens.
2.  Meanwhile, reheat the corn.
3.  To serve the partridge you can either present them whole or remove the bacon and carve off each breast and leg as you would for a chicken. The bacon can be cut into two or three pieces and used to garnish the dish.
4.  Place a spoonful of the honeyed corn on the plates and arrange the partridge and bacon over that. Garnish with some sautéed greens and dress with the fig vinaigrette.

# Free-range duck breast glazed with spiced honey caramel, served with quince puree and toasted walnuts

There has been much media attention recently concerning the lack of 'animal husbandry' in the production of duck for the supermarkets. As ever, I urge you to source free-range duck! This recipe is inspired by one of Alain Senderens' (French master chef of Lucas Carton fame) signature dishes (Canard Apicius) that is based on a 2000 year-old Roman recipe. The rich duck marries really well with the sweet, spicy, aromatic honey caramel. Be careful when handling the caramel as it will be very hot and take care not to over cook it. I have specified a full bodied wine for the making of the sauce as this will result in a deeply coloured and rich finish. I like to accompany this with a simple salad dressed with a little walnut oil and lemon juice.
Serves 6

For the duck breasts & spiced caramel:
6 free-range duck breasts
200g/ 7oz clear wild flower honey
3 tbsp coriander seeds
3 tbsp cumin seeds
1 tbsp sesame seeds
1 tbsp fennel seeds
½ tbsp dried rosemary
½ tbsp dried thyme
½ tbsp green peppercorns
1 tsp ground cinnamon
½ tsp ground cloves
½ tsp ground star anise

100g/ 3 ½oz walnuts, toasted
Sea salt & black pepper

For the quince puree:
3 quinces
½ cinnamon stick
2 tbsp castor sugar
½ orange

For the sauce:
1 bottle full bodied red wine
1 onion, chopped
1 garlic clove, crushed
1lt/ 1 ¾ pints chicken stock
½ cinnamon stick
75g/ 2 ½ oz unsalted butter,

To prepare the quince puree:
1. Peel, quarter and core the quince. Cover with water in a suitable sized saucepan and add the cinnamon, sugar and orange. Bring to a simmer and cook until the quince is soft. Remove the quince to a blender and puree until smooth. Season with a touch of salt and reserve.

To prepare the sauce:
1. Add the wine to a heavy based pan with the onion and garlic and *reduce* by half.
2. Add the chicken stock and cinnamon stick and reduce by a further two thirds.
3. Turn the heat to low and gradually whisk in the butter until completely *emulsified*.
4. Pass through a fine sieve and reserve.

To prepare the duck and caramel:

Pre-heat the oven to 220°C/ 425°F/ Gas mark 7.

1. Heat a large non-stick frying pan until very hot. Season the duck breasts and seal fat side down. Drain off the excess fat and continue to cook until the fat on the duck breast is very well caramelised. This may take up to 10 minutes.
2. Remove the duck from the pan and drain on kitchen paper. Place in a baking tray, fat side facing up.
3. In a clean heavy based pan, combine the honey with all the spices. Cook over a low heat to begin with until the spices are fully incorporated and then increase the heat and cook to an amber caramel. Quickly place the base of the pan in a sink of cold water to stop the cooking process.
4. Spoon the caramel over the duck breasts ensuring an even layer of coverage.
5. Place the duck in the centre of the oven and cook for 5 minutes. Remove and leave to *rest* for 5 minutes.

To finish and serve:

1. Gently re-heat the sauce and quince puree in saucepans.
2. Slice each duck breast into three or five slices and fan across the bottom of six warmed serving plates.
3. Place a couple of dessert spoonfuls or *quenelles* of the quince puree above the duck and spoon a little sauce around the duck.
4. Sprinkle with the walnuts and serve.

The spiced honey caramel
making process

# Supreme of pheasant with bacon and celery farce
# and a celery sauce

I first prepared this dish in the late 1990's at a restaurant I worked at with my brother (Robert Thompson – awarded 1 Michelin star, 9/10 Good Food Guide and 4 AA Rosettes in 2006). This recipe only calls for the supreme of the pheasant, but you could utilise the legs and carcass for a pheasant pie or a rich pheasant soup. The pheasant supreme is kept moist by the farce, and the breadcrumbs provide a nice crispy coating. You could serve this with some steamed green vegetables and potatoes braised with chicken stock, garlic and fresh herbs. Serves 6

For the pheasant supreme:
6 Supremes of pheasant, skinless
6 rashers thick cut organic bacon
6 sticks celery, peeled & finely chopped
1 tsp thyme leaves
1 onion, finely chopped
½ garlic clove, peeled & finely crushed
450g/ 1lb breadcrumbs (page 271)
3 free-range organic eggs
100ml/ 3 ½ fl oz milk
200g/ 7oz plain flour

Deep-fried celery leaves (page 174)
6 tbsp vegetable oil
50g/ 2oz unsalted butter
Sea salt & black pepper

For the celery sauce:
1 head celery, washed & trimmed
1 onion, finely chopped
1 garlic clove, peeled & finely crushed
300ml/ 11fl oz white wine
1lt/ 1 ¾ pints chicken stock (see basics)
250ml/ 9fl oz double cream
2 tbsp snipped chives

To prepare the pheasant:
1. Trim the pheasant supremes and remove the mini-fillet/mignon on the underside of the supreme.
2. Cut the mini fillets into 5mm/ ¼″ dice.
3. Cut the bacon into 5mm/ ¼″ dice and combine in a bowl with the diced pheasant.
4. Heat 2 tbsp of the oil in a non-stick frying pan and *sweat* the onion, garlic and celery until softened. Cool.
5. Mix together the diced meat and cooked vegetables and add the thyme leaves. Season to taste.
6. Divide the mixture into six equal portions and press them onto the underside of the pheasant Supremes to form an even layer. Chill for 20 minutes.
7. Whisk together the eggs and milk in a bowl.
8. Season the flour in another bowl.
9. Carefully coat the pheasant in the flour, then the egg and then finally the breadcrumbs. Chill again for 20 minutes.

To prepare the celery sauce:
1. Roughly chop the celery.
2. Heat 1 tbsp of the oil in a saucepan and sweat the onion, garlic and celery together until softened.
3. Add the white wine and *reduce* by half.
4. Next, add the chicken stock, bring to the boil and then simmer for 15 minutes.
5. Finally, add the double cream and simmer for another 5 minutes.
6. Transfer to a blender and puree until smooth. Pass through a fine sieve and season to taste. Reserve.

To finish and serve:
Pre-heat the oven to 200°C/ 400°F/ Gas mark 6.
1. Heat the remaining oil and butter in a large non-stick frying pan and gently sauté the pheasant until lightly coloured on both sides.
2. Transfer to a baking tray and cook in the oven for 10-12 minutes. Don't over cook it or the meat will be dry.
3. Remove from the oven and *rest* for 5 minutes.
4. Meanwhile, re-heat the sauce and any vegetable garnishes you may have prepared.
5. Slice each pheasant supreme into three or five slices and fan across each plate.
6. Add the chives to the sauce and pour the sauce around the pheasant. Scatter over the crispy celery leaves and serve with the vegetables served in separate side dishes.

Supreme of pheasant with bacon and celery farce and a celery sauce

# Loin of local lamb cooked in salt pastry, with wilted red and green chard, tomato and chilli chutney and lamb jus

Ideal for later in the season when the lambs are bigger, thus yielding a larger best end and loin. For this dish I would buy a whole best end and remove the loins myself. The bones would then form the basis for my stock and sauce, and the mini-fillets could be used in a stir-fry or flash-fried for a salad. If you don't feel confident enough to do this yourself, ask your butcher to prepare the lamb. Contrary to what you may think, cooking the lamb in salt pastry does not make it salty, but keeps the juice and flavour in the meat perfectly. Tender chard stems and leaves compliment the lamb well, as does the tomato chutney that you should have in storage from the summer glut.
Serves 6

For the lamb and salt pastry:
2 whole best ends of lamb, loins removed & trimmed
1 tbsp thyme & rosemary leaves
1 tbsp extra virgin olive oil
1kg/ 2lb 2oz plain flour
450g/ 1lb coarse sea salt
200ml/ 7fl oz water
1 beaten egg

For the lamb jus:
1kg/ 2lb 2oz lamb bones, chopped
1 garlic clove, peeled & crushed
2 carrots, peeled & sliced
2 sticks celery, sliced
2 onions, roughly chopped
½ bottle red wine
2lts/ 2 ½ pints water
1 bouquet garni (see basics)

For the wilted chards:
450g/ 1lb red & green chard, washed & trimmed into 10cm/ 4″ lengths

6 tbsp tomato & chilli chutney (page 154)
2 tbsp extra virgin olive oil
75g/ 2 ½oz unsalted butter, diced
Sea salt & black pepper

To prepare the lamb jus:
1. Heat a large heavy based saucepan.
2. Add the lamb bones and pan roast until well caramelised.
3. Remove the bones and drain on kitchen paper.
4. Add the garlic, carrots, celery and onion to the pan and *sauté* until golden brown.
5. Add the red wine and *reduce* by half. Add the water, bring to the boil, *skim* and then simmer slowly for 2 hours.
6. Pass through a fine sieve, return to a clean pan, bring to the boil and reduce by half. Reserve.

To prepare the salt pastry and lamb:

1. Combine the flour and sea salt together in a bowl and add the water. Knead to a smooth dough and chill for 20 minutes.
2. On a lightly floured surface, divide the dough into six equal portions and roll them out to a thickness of approximately 5mm/ ¼" and about 15cm x 15cm/ 6"x 6". Chill.
3. Remove the fine layer of sinew from the lamb fillet, season, and rub with the olive oil and then the herbs.
4. Lay each piece of lamb at the bottom of the pastry and brush the edges of the pastry with the beaten egg. Fold over the pastry and seal all the edges firmly to form a neat parcel.
5. Transfer to a baking tray and chill until required.

To finish and serve:

Pre-heat the oven to 220°C/ 425°F/ Gas mark 7.

1. Place the lamb/pastry parcels in the oven and bake for 15 (medium rare)-20 (medium to well done) minutes depending on your preference of cooking degree.
2. Heat a large saucepan 5 minutes before the lamb is ready.
3. Add the chard with a dash of water and cover with a lid for 1 minute.
4. Remove the lid; the chard should have wilted but still have retained its form and texture. Season.
5. Reheat the lamb jus, and whisk in the butter slowly.
6. Open the salt pastry parcels, remove the lamb and slice thinly. Discard the pastry
7. On six warmed serving plates, arrange neat piles of the chard and lay the sliced lamb on top. Place a spoonful of the tomato chutney on the side and spoon over some lamb jus.
8. Finish with a drizzle of the olive oil and serve.

# Braised onions with cèpe duxelle, onion cream sauce and cèpe oil

As well as making a good vegetarian main course, I would also recommend this as an accompaniment to a roasted beef fillet or roast organic chicken. It requires a little care when separating the layers of onion for stuffing. As with the salad of cèpes and prawns on page 168, you could swap the cèpes for chestnut mushrooms.
Serves 6

For the onions & cèpe *duxelle*:
18 medium onions
1kg/ 2lb 2oz cèpes, cleaned & trimmed
1 garlic clove, peeled & crushed
1 tbsp thyme leaves
100g/ 3 ½fl oz fresh white breadcrumbs
2 tbsp vegetable oil

Cèpe oil (see basics)
Salt & black pepper
2 tbsp snipped chives

For the onion cream sauce:
Trimmings from the 18 onions
1 garlic clove, peeled & crushed
1 tbsp vegetable oil
200ml/ 7fl oz white wine
500ml/ 18fl oz veg stock (see basics)
4 tbsp crème fraîche

To prepare the onions and duxelle:
1. Bring a large saucepan of water to the boil and cook the onions for 3-4 minutes until they start to soften. Remove and *refresh* in iced water. Drain.
2. Carefully peel the onions and remove the top and root.
3. Working carefully, remove one of the outer layers from the onion in one piece.
4. · Roughly chop the remainder of the onion and use for the sauce.
5. Chop the cèpes very finely.
6. Heat the oil in a large non-stick frying pan and fry the cèpes and onion until lightly coloured. Add the thyme, breadcrumbs and season.
7. Carefully stuff the duxelle into the onions. Reserve.

To prepare the onion cream sauce:
1. Heat the oil in a saucepan and *sweat* the onion trimmings and garlic.
2. Add the white wine and *reduce* by half.
3. Add the vegetable stock, bring to a boil and simmer for 20 minutes.
4. Add the crème fraîche, transfer to a blender and puree until smooth. Season and reserve.

To finish and serve:
1. Prepare a steamer.
2. Re-heat the onions in the steamer and re-heat the sauce.
3. In six warmed shallow serving bowls, pour in some of the onion sauce and place three onions on top. Drizzle with cèpe oil, sprinkle with chives and serve.

# Baked pumpkin and cinnamon cheesecake

Based on the classic baked New York style cheesecake, this is a really homely and warming dessert that you could serve with a simple seasonal fruit salad or some dried fruit compote which you can find a recipe for on page 272.
Serves 6-8

300g/ 10oz pumpkin flesh, roughly chopped
1 stick cinnamon
4 free-range organic eggs
100g/ 3 ½oz castor sugar
350g/ 12oz marscapone cheese
1 vanilla pod, split & seeds scraped out
½ tsp ground cinnamon
Grated zest & juice of 1 organic orange

150g/ 5oz wholewheat digestive biscuits
100g/ 3 ½oz organic oats
100g/ 3 ½oz unsalted butter

Butter for greasing

Pre-heat the oven to 150°C/ 300°F/ Gas mark 2.
1. Crush the digestive biscuits until they resemble coarse breadcrumbs. Combine with the oats in a bowl.
2. Melt the butter and mix with the biscuits.
3. Lightly grease and line a 20cm/ 8″ deep-sided cake tin with a removable base. Press the biscuit mix firmly and evenly into the base.
4. Place the pumpkin and cinnamon stick in a saucepan and cover with water. Bring to a simmer and cook until the pumpkin is soft. Drain, remove the cinnamon stick and chill.
5. Using an electric mixer, whisk together the eggs and castor sugar in a bowl until they have tripled in volume. Stir in the marscapone cheese followed by the vanilla seeds, cinnamon and the orange.
6. Puree the pumpkin until smooth and fold into the cheesecake mix.
7. Pour into the cake tin and place in the centre of the oven.
8. Cook for approximately 1 ¼ hours until the centre of the cheesecake is just set.
9. Remove from the oven and leave to fully set at room temperature for about 2 hours.
10. To serve, remove from the tin using a palette knife to assist you, slice and accompany with your chosen garnish.

# Poached dessert apples with five spices and toasted hazelnut crème fraîche

If you have an apple tree in your garden this is an excellent recipe for a quick, tasty dessert that can be prepared in advance or eaten immediately. You may vary the spices to suit your own taste, and of course substitute the crème fraîche for whipped double cream or clotted cream if you so desire. You will be left with some wonderfully fragrant cooking liquor from this dish. I suggest that you make an apple jelly by adding seven leaves (per 450ml/ 1 pint) of soaked and melted gelatine to the liquor, and then setting it in the fridge. Served with some cinnamon flavoured shortbread, this is another delicious autumnal dessert.
Serves 6

12 apples such as Ellison's Orange or Ribston Pippin , rinsed & cored
5 cloves
2 star anise
1 cinnamon stick
5 green cardamom pods
1 vanilla pod, split
Juice and grated *zest* of 1 organic lemon
1lt/ 1 ¾ pints fresh apple juice
100g/ 3 ½oz soft brown sugar

2 tbsp chopped hazelnuts, toasted
6 tbsp crème fraîche

To prepare the apples:
1. Cut each apple into three even slices through the cross section.
2. Combine in a saucepan with the spices, lemon, apple juice and sugar.
3. Bring to a gentle simmer and cook until the apples are tender but still retaining their shape.
4. Remove from the heat and leave to *infuse* at room temperature for a minimum of 20 minutes but ideally a couple of hours.

To finish and serve:
1. Mix the hazelnuts and crème fraîche together in a bowl.
2. Spoon the slices of apple into six serving bowls and spoon over some of the cooking liquor.
3. Top with a spoonful of crème fraîche and serve.

# Pears steeped in red wine and ginger-rosemary

This is an excellent way of preserving pears for future use. I like to use Comice, Catallic or Packham pears for this recipe as they hold their shape very well. You could enjoy these by themselves, or perhaps top the pears with a little Roquefort cheese and toasted walnuts. You can adjust the recipe quantities to suit your own requirements.
Serves 6

9 pears, slightly under-ripe
200g/ 7oz castor sugar
1 bottle fruity & spicy red wine
2 large sprigs of ginger-rosemary
Grated *zest* & juice of 1 orange

1. Peel, halve and remove the core from the pears.
2. In a large saucepan, bring the sugar and wine to the boil and simmer for 5 minutes.
3. Add the pears, ginger-rosemary and orange.
4. Add water to just cover the pears and bring back to a simmer.
5. Cook gently until the pears are tender.
6. Transfer the pears to a large sterilised kilner jar and pour in the cooking liquor.
7. Seal the lid by steaming the jar or by cooking in a *Bain Marie* for 20 minutes.
8. Remove and leave to cool.
9. Leave the pears to *steep* in a cool, dry place for at least one week before eating.

# Pear and almond tart with marmalade ice cream and rose water sauce

This dish is based on the classic 'Tarte Bordalue'. I have given the dessert a twist by serving some home-made marmalade ice cream with it, as well as a rose water scented sauce. These complement the pear and almond flavours in the tart.
Serves 6-8

For the pastry:
50g/ 2oz ground almonds
175g/ 6oz plain organic flour
125g/ 4oz unsalted butter
75g/ 2 ½oz icing sugar
1 free-range organic egg yolk
Pinch of salt
1 vanilla pod, split & de-seeded

For the ice cream:
250ml/ 9fl oz whole organic milk
250ml/ 9fl oz double cream
6 free-range organic egg yolks
100g/ 3 ½ oz castor sugar
3 tbsp home-made marmalade

Toasted flaked almonds to garnish

For the almond filling & pears:
100g/ 3 ½oz unsalted butter
50g/ 2oz ground almonds
100g/ 3 ½oz castor sugar
50g/ 2oz plain organic flour
2 free-range organic eggs
½ tsp almond essence
4 pears, peeled, halved & cored
1lt/1 ¾ pints water
300g/ 10oz castor sugar

For the rose water sauce:
500ml/ 18fl oz fresh orange juice
100g/ 3 ½ oz castor sugar
2 tbsp rose water essence

To prepare the pastry:
1. Soften the butter and cream together with the icing sugar in a bowl. Add the egg yolk and mix well. Add the salt and vanilla seeds.
2. Sift the almonds and flour together and work into the butter. Gently mix to a smooth dough, wrap in Clingfilm and chill for a couple of hours.
3. Grease and lightly flour a 20cm/ 8″ flan/tart tin.
4. Roll out the pastry on a lightly floured surface to an even thickness of 4-5mm/ ¼″. Transfer to the tin and press into the edges and sides. Trim the overlapping pastry edges to within 3cm/ 1″ of the tin edge. You can trim the pastry neatly after cooking. Chill again for 30 minutes.
5. Pre-heat the oven to 190°C/ 375°F/ Gas mark 5.
6. Fill the pastry case with baking beans and '*blind bake*' for about 20-25 minutes until the pastry is cooked through and lightly coloured. Remove and cool.

To prepare the crème anglaise for the ice cream:
1. In a heavy based saucepan, bring the cream and milk to the boil.
2. Meanwhile, whisk the egg yolks and sugar together in a bowl.
3. Pour the milk and cream onto the eggs and mix well.
4. Return to a medium heat in a clean saucepan and cook gently, stirring constantly, until it thickens enough to coat the back of a spoon. Transfer the pan immediately to iced water to stop the cooking process and to chill.
5. Add the marmalade and mix well. If your marmalade has chunky peel, you can puree the crème anglaise mix a little.
6. Transfer the chilled crème anglaise to an ice cream machine and churn. Freeze until required.

To prepare the sauce:
1. Boil together the orange juice and sugar until reduced by three quarters in volume. Add the rose water and chill until required.

To prepare the almond filling (frangipane) and pears:
Pre-heat the oven to 200°C/ 400°F/ Gas mark 6.
1. Bring the litre of water and 300g/ 10oz of sugar to the boil in a saucepan and boil for 5 minutes. Add the pear halves, then simmer until tender and remove from the liquid to cool a little.
2. Cream the butter and sugar together in a bowl until light and fluffy.
3. Gradually mix in the beaten eggs and then fold in the almonds and flour.
4. Add the almond essence.
5. Spread the almond mix over the base of the pastry case and arrange the pear halves on top.
6. Bake in the centre of the oven for 30-35 minutes until the frangipane has risen and lightly coloured. Remove and cool.
7. Take 300ml/10fl oz of the pear poaching liquid and *reduce* by half in a saucepan. Glaze the tart with this syrup to give it a glossy shine. Remove from the flan tin and trim the edges of the pastry neatly with scissors.

To finish and serve:
1. Cut the pear and almond tart into six or eight slices and arrange on the serving plates with some ice cream and rose water sauce. Sprinkle with toasted almonds and serve.

Pear and almond tart
with marmalade ice
cream and rose
water sauce

Tart Tatin of apples with cider ice cream and thyme caramel

# Tart Tatin of apples with cider ice cream and thyme caramel

An apple Tart Tatin really showcases autumn. Ideally, I would prepare this dessert using a large shallow copper pan, but you could use a similar ovenproof pan.
Serves 6

For the ice cream:
250ml/ 9fl oz whole organic milk
250ml/ 9fl oz double cream
6 free-range egg yolks
100g/ 3 ½ oz castor sugar
Grated *zest* of 1 organic lemon
200ml/ 7fl oz sweet cider

For the Tart Tatin:
6 apples such as Cox's Pomona
300g/ 10oz castor sugar
50g/ 2oz unsalted butter
1 tbsp thyme leaves
300g/ 10oz fresh puff pastry (see basics)

To prepare the ice cream:
1. In a heavy based saucepan, bring the milk and cream to the boil.
2. Meanwhile whisk the egg yolks and sugar together in a bowl and mix in the cider and lemon zest.
3. Whisk the milk onto the eggs and return to a medium heat in a clean saucepan.
4. Cook gently until it thickens enough to coat the back of a spoon.
5. Chill the pan immediately over iced water.
6. Churn in an ice cream machine and then freeze until required.

To prepare the Tart Tatin:
Pre-heat the oven to 220°C/ 425°F/ Gas mark 7.
1. Peel, halve and core the apples.
2. In the copper or ovenproof pan, add the sugar and cook over a low heat until the sugar has completely melted. Increase the heat and cook to a deep amber coloured caramel.
3. Stir in the butter and the thyme leaves.
4. Arrange the apple halves in the caramel leaving a 2 ½cm/ 1" gap around the edge.
5. Roll out the puff pastry to an even thickness and cut out a circle 2 ½cm/ 1" larger then the diameter of the pan.
6. Lay the pastry on top of the apples.
7. Turn down the pastry and tuck around the base of the apples and caramel.
8. Prick the top of the pastry with a fork several times.
9. Transfer to the oven and cook for 30-35 minutes.
10. Remove from the oven and turn out the Tart Tatin using a similar sized plate or baking tray to achieve this. Be careful not to burn yourself with the hot caramel.
11. The result should be crisp, caramelised pastry around the edge with beautifully caramelised cooked apples in the centre. Leave to rest for 5 minutes.

To finish and serve:
1. Simply slice the Tart Tatin, accompany it with cider ice cream and serve.

# Medlar fruit baked with cream and cinnamon, served with oat biscuits

Medlar fruit are notoriously difficult to find, the exception being in a few private gardens. The Medlar is a small dark green/brown fruit with petals arranged around its flattish top. It is picked after a hard frost, and then kept cool until the pulp softens inside the fruit; this is called bletting and produces a fruit with a sweet, wine like flavour. If you are fortunate enough to have a Medlar tree in your garden, then you could try out this dish for your discerning guests.
Serves 6

For the baked fruit:
1kg/ 2lb 2oz Medlar fruit
100g/ 3 ½ oz demerara sugar
1 tsp ground cinnamon
25g/ 1oz whole almonds
350ml/ 12fl oz double cream
3 free-range organic eggs

For the oat biscuits:
100g/ 3 ½ oz unsalted butter, softened
50g/ 2oz castor sugar
2 tbsp organic clear honey
175g/ 6oz organic oats
50g/ 2oz toasted desiccated coconut
55g/ 2oz wholewheat organic flour

To prepare the oat biscuits:
Pre-heat the oven to 180°C/ 350°F/ Gas mark 4.
1. Cream the butter, sugar and honey together in a bowl until light and fluffy.
2. Add the oats, coconut and flour then mix well to a smooth paste.
3. Roll out to an even thickness of 5mm/ ¼" and cut out 8cm/ 3" circles. Repeat to use all of the biscuit mix.
4. Lay the circles onto a greased baking tray and bake in the centre of the oven until lightly coloured. Remove and cool on a wire rack.

To prepare the baked fruit:
Pre-heat the oven to 190°C/ 375°F/ Gas mark 5.
1. Scoop out the flesh of the Medlar fruit using a small spoon or a melon baller.
2. Whisk together the cream and eggs.
3. Spoon the Medlar flesh into six large ramekins and sprinkle with the sugar, cinnamon and almonds.
4. Pour the cream and egg mixture over the fruit.
5. Transfer the ramekins to a baking tray and cook in the centre of the oven for approximately 25 minutes or until the cream is just set.
6. Remove from the oven and cool for 5 minutes.

To finish and serve:
1. Serve the ramekins of baked fruit with a few oat biscuits.

The Essence - Contemporary recipes inspired by a traditional kitchen garden

# Poached quince with honey and ginger and a lightly spiced baba

This is a really comforting, homely dessert using another uncommon fruit. Quince is native to the Middle East and some Mediterranean areas, particularly Turkey. It is also quite common in traditional English walled kitchen gardens. The quince has a strong perfume-like aroma and a bitter flesh that needs to be cooked to realise its full potential. I find that cooking it slowly with honey, ginger and some sweet wine works very well.
Serves 6

For the poached quince:
3 large quinces
3 tbsp clear honey
10g/ ⅓ oz root ginger, peeled & finely chopped
350ml/ 12floz sweet dessert wine
1 vanilla pod, split
5 cardamom pods
2 cloves
¼ nutmeg, grated

250g/ 9oz castor sugar
750ml/ 1 ½ pints water
Crystallised lemon & orange peel

For the *baba*:
200g/ 7oz strong organic white flour
5g/ ¼ oz fresh yeast
125ml/ 4fl oz whole organic milk
2 free-range organic eggs
50g/ 2oz unsalted butter
10g/ ⅓ oz castor sugar
pinch of salt
1 tsp ground mixed spice

To prepare the baba:
Pre-heat the oven to 220°C/ 425°F/ Gas mark 7.

1.  Sift the flour, salt and mixed spice into a bowl.
2.  Warm the milk and mix a little with the yeast and sugar.
3.  Make a well in the centre of the flour and add the yeast. Sprinkle the yeast with a little flour, cover the bowl and leave in a warm place until the yeast begins to *ferment*.
4.  Pour in the rest of the warm milk, beaten eggs and mix to a smooth dough.
5.  Return to the bowl and mix in the diced butter. Leave to *prove* in a warm place until it has doubled in volume (Fig.1).
6.  *Knock back* the dough and transfer to greased Dariole moulds or six smaller individual moulds.
7.  Prove the dough again until it fills the moulds and then bake in the oven for 15-20 minutes (dependent on mould size).
8.  Once cooked (test by inserting a skewer; it should come out clean), turn out of the moulds.
9.  Boil the castor sugar and water together in a saucepan for 5 minutes and then soak the baba in the syrup for at least an hour (Fig.2). Reserve the finished baba at room temperature until required.

To prepare the poached quince:

1.  Peel the quinces and quarter them. Remove the core and place in a large saucepan.
2.  Add the remaining spices, honey and wine and cover with water.
3.  Bring to a simmer and *poach* gently until the quince is tender throughout but not falling apart.
4.  Remove from the heat and leave to cool.

To finish and serve:

1.  Remove the quince from the cooking liquor and cut into bite sized pieces.
2.  Take about 500ml/ 18 fl oz of the cooking liquor and quickly *reduce* by half over a high heat.
3.  Arrange the baba and quince on six serving plates and spoon a little of the reduced liquor around. Finish with some of the orange and lemon peel and serve.

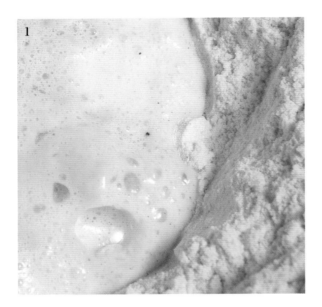

# Apple, onion and thyme chutney

I like to store the chutneys that I prepare in different sized jars. They are then ready to be used or given away as gifts as required. Obviously, chutney matures in depth of flavour over time, so it's best to leave it to stand for at least a month before enjoying it.

3kg/ 6lb 6oz Bramley apples
2 kg/ 4 ¼ lb onions, finely chopped
6 garlic cloves, peeled & finely crushed
6 sprigs of thyme
1lt/ 1 ¾ pints white wine vinegar
450g/ 1lb demerara sugar

2 tsp ground mixed spice
1 tsp ground cumin
1 tsp ground coriander
Sea salt & black pepper
Selection of sterilised jars & lids

To prepare the chutney:
1. Peel, core and cut the apples into 1cm/ ½" dice.
2. In a large saucepan, bring the vinegar and sugar to the boil and cook for approximately 5 minutes.
3. Stir in the onions and garlic and simmer for 5 minutes.
4. Add the apples, thyme and spices, cover and simmer for 30 minutes. The apples and onions should have softened but still have retained some of their shape. The chutney should have a good sweet and sour balance in taste.
5. Season the chutney.
6. Warm the jars in a low heat oven and transfer the chutney into the jars whilst still hot.
7. Cover the jars with lids and store in a cool, dry place until required.
8. Refrigerate after opening.

# Caramelised onion compote with fennel seeds

This compote makes a good accompaniment to grilled fish such as salmon and turbot, as well as sautéed and grilled lamb cutlets.

2kg/ 4 ¼ lb onions, finely sliced
4 garlic cloves, peeled & finely crushed
4 tbsp olive oil
500ml/ 18fl oz white wine
100g/ 3 ½ oz demerara sugar
2 tbsp fennel seeds
Sea salt & black pepper

Small sterilised jars & lids

To prepare the chutney:
1. Heat the olive oil in a large saucepan and add the onions and garlic.
2. Cook over a medium to high heat until softened.
3. Add the white wine and *reduce* by half over a high heat.
4. Add the sugar and continue to cook until the onions are evenly caramelised and have taken on a rich golden colour.
5. Add the fennel seeds and cook for a further 2 minutes.
6. Season the compote.
7. Warm the jars in a low heat oven and transfer the compote to the jars whilst still hot.
8. Cover the jars with lids and store in a cool, dry place for up to three months.
9. Refrigerate once opened.

# Spiced vegetable chutney

You can use your own selection of vegetables in this chutney. I have simply listed the produce that I prefer to use.

Makes about 2 ½ kg/ 5lb:

3 large onions, peeled & chopped into 1cm/ ½" dice
6 garlic cloves, peeled & finely crushed
5 large carrots, peeled & finely sliced
1 head celery, washed, trimmed & finely sliced
2 medium beetroots, peeled & chopped into 1cm/ ½" dice
1 large cauliflower, washed & cut into small florets
4 long fresh red chillies, sliced
1 tbsp minced lemongrass
1 tbsp root ginger, finely chopped
2 tsp coriander seeds
2 tsp cumin seeds
1 tsp ground cinnamon
2 tsp mustard seeds
6 cloves
1lt/ 1 ¾ pints white wine vinegar
350g/ 12oz preserving sugar
Sea salt & black pepper

1. Combine all the ingredients except the sugar in a large preserving pan. Cover and simmer for 1 ½ hours until most of the liquid has been driven off and the vegetables are soft.
2. Stir in the sugar and cook gently until the sugar has dissolved.
3. Increase the heat and boil rapidly until the chutney is thick.
4. Season the chutney and pour into warm, clean jars. Cover with a lid, label and store in a cool, dark place.

# Aromatic quince preserve

This is a variation on quince cheese, and is excellent when served with cold meats and game.

12 quinces
1 tsp ground allspice
1 tsp ground cinnamon
¼ grated nutmeg
3 cloves
1 star anise
½ tsp ground ginger
350ml/ 12fl oz water
450g/ 1lb granulated sugar per 500ml/ 18fl oz quince puree

1. Peel, quarter and core the quinces.
2. Place in a preserving pan with the water and spices.
3. Cover and simmer until the quinces are soft. Crush the quinces until well mashed and pass through a fine sieve.
4. Measure the puree back into the pan and add the required amount of sugar.
5. Cook gently until the sugar has dissolved and then increase the heat.
6. Boil the puree, stirring throughout, until you can pull a line through the puree in the pan.
7. Transfer to warm, clean jars.
8. Cover with a lid, label and store in a cool, dark place.

# Winter

The long, dark winter months invite you to enjoy rich and warming food. I like to think of this season as an opportunity in which to experiment a little with those tried and tested flavour combinations, whilst still preparing satisfying and elegant recipes from all those fantastic roots, tubers and brassicas. You will also be able to enjoy all of the jams, chutneys and pickles that you prepared over the summer and autumn months. Dishes such as a winter salad of roasted and spiced vegetables combined with a piquant dressing, some Artisan cheese and a few toasted nuts compare equally well to the salad you may prepare during the summer. The game season is in full swing by now, giving you the chance to marry interesting preparations of vegetables with venison, pigeon and rabbit to name but a few.

The ever faithful leeks, that last well into February, make an appearance on pages 219 and 238. Leeks also make fantastic soup with the addition of perhaps some nutmeg, truffle, blue cheese or bacon. As well as leeks, you will find recipes including carrots, parsnips, swede, beetroot, winter cabbage, sprouting broccoli, potatoes, salsify, curly kale, chicory, Brussels sprouts, chestnuts, apples and pears.

# Fricassee of greens, walnuts and onion compote with sautéed pigeon breast

This is a colourful starter, full of different tastes, textures and aromas. I would serve this as a starter at an autumnal dinner party. Walnuts are available during October and November. Walnuts can be blanched and then refreshed in iced water to remove their bitter skin. I have suggested a rich red wine reduction which complements the fricassee and the pigeon.
Serves 6

**For the fricassee:**
250g/ 9oz mixed greens & curly kale, washed
200g/ 7oz onion compote (see basics)
100g/ 3 ½ oz fresh or dried walnuts
2 tbsp olive oil
1 garlic clove, peeled & crushed
3 sticks celery, washed & cut into julienne
300ml/ 11fl oz vegetable stock (see basics)
100ml/ 3 ½ fl oz double cream
1 tsp thyme leaves

Sea salt & black pepper

**For the red wine reduction:**
1 bottle red wine
1 tbsp demerara sugar

**For the pigeon:**
6 pigeon breasts, skinless
1 tbsp vegetable oil
25g/ 1oz unsalted butter

To prepare the red wine reduction:
1. Simply *reduce* the wine and sugar together in a saucepan until you are left with a syrupy, glossy sauce. Season and reserve.

To prepare the fricassee:
1. Remove any particularly fibrous stalk from the greens and kale. *Blanch* in a large saucepan of boiling salted water and then *refresh* in iced water and drain well.
2. Heat the olive oil in a large frying pan and sweat the garlic and celery until soft.
3. Stir in the onion compote and walnuts and add the vegetable stock. Simmer for 5 minutes and then add the cream. Continue to cook for another 5 minutes.
4. Add the thyme leaves and stir in the greens and kale. Season and reserve.

To finish and serve:
1. Heat the vegetable oil in a non-stick frying pan.
2. Season the pigeon breasts and fry them for 3 minutes on each side.
3. Add the butter and cook for another minute.
4. Remove the pigeon and *rest* for 5 minutes.
5. Re-heat the fricassee and spoon it equally into the centre of six warmed serving plates.
6. Slice the pigeon breasts and lay them across the fricassee.
7. Spoon a little red wine reduction around the plate and serve.

Fricassee of greens, walnuts and onion compote with sautéed pigeon breast

# Gratin of salsify, Prosciutto ham and capers with a free-range organic egg

You could be forgiven for being put off by the look of salsify in its natural state, but I assure you it is worth the effort and time taken to prepare it. Salsify or Scorzonera is becoming more commonly available, especially in farmers' markets, and you may well have some growing in your kitchen garden. Being a very muddy vegetable and prone to an uneven surface it requires thorough cleaning before use.
Serves 6

3 tbsp olive oil
1 garlic clove, peeled & crushed
1 onion, finely sliced
750g/ 1lb 11oz salsify, washed, peeled & cut into 6cm/ 2 ½" lengths
200g/ 7oz Prosciutto ham, thinly sliced & cut into thin strips
2 tbsp baby capers
200ml/ 7oz white wine
250ml/ 9fl oz double cream
1 tbsp parsley, washed & finely chopped
100g/ 3 ½ oz organic mature cheddar cheese

6 free-range organic eggs
White wine vinegar for poaching

Olive oil
Fresh herbs to garnish

Sea salt & black pepper

1. Cook the salsify in boiling salted water until just tender. *Refresh* in iced water and drain.
2. Heat the oil in a frying pan and *sweat* the garlic and onion.
3. Add the salsify and cook for a further 3 minutes.
4. Add the white wine and *reduce* by half.
5. Next, add the cream, ham and capers and simmer gently for 5 minutes.
6. Finally, add the parsley, season and reserve.
7. *Poach* the eggs in simmering water with a touch of vinegar until the white has just set. Refer to page 29 for description on how best to achieve this.
8. Pre-heat the grill to a high temperature.
9. Spoon the salsify and sauce into six small ovenproof dishes such as '*cocotte*' or '*sur le plat*' dishes. Top with the poached egg and sprinkle with the cheese.
10. *Gratinate* under the hot grill until lightly coloured.
11. Drizzle with olive oil, garnish with a few herbs and serve.

Gratin of salsify, Prosciutto ham
and capers with a free-range
organic egg

# Braised leeks with truffles, vegetable brunoise and truffle butter croutons

Here is a dish that combines the common and humble vegetable with the exquisite truffle. This is one of the first composed vegetable accompaniments that I prepared during my formative training period. It would serve well as a stand alone starter or as a side dish to accompany roast free-range chicken or lamb. White truffle oil varies greatly in quality. I recommend that you source an individual Artisan product, and it's better to spend a little extra money on this.

Serves 6

For the braised leeks:
6 leeks, trimmed & well washed
1 garlic clove, peeled & finely crushed
1 onion, finely chopped
2 carrots, peeled, cut into *brunoise*
3 sticks celery, cut into *brunoise*
2 courgettes cut into *brunoise*
1 bouquet garni (see basics)
500ml/ 18fl oz vegetable stock (see basics)
1 tbsp white truffle oil
1 tbsp olive oil
2 small truffles, thinly sliced

Sea salt & black pepper
Chopped fresh herbs to garnish

For the truffle butter croutons:
50g/ 2oz salted butter
1 small truffle, finely chopped
1 tsp white truffle oil
2 tsp snipped chives
6 slices soda bread

For the braised leeks:
1. Cut each leek into three equal lengths.
2. Heat the olive and truffle oil in a frying pan and gently *sweat* the leeks for 3-4 minutes.
3. Add the garlic, onion, carrot and celery and continue to sweat for 3-4 minutes.
4. Add the courgettes, the vegetable stock and the bouquet garni. Sprinkle with the truffle, season and simmer for 15-20 minutes until the leeks are cooked through, but not mushy.
5. Check the seasoning and reserve.

For the truffle butter croutons:
1. Soften the butter in a microwave and mix with the chopped truffle, truffle oil and chives in a bowl. Check the seasoning.
2. Cut three small circles from each slice of bread and toast lightly. Cool.
3. Spread the croutons with the butter and reserve.

To finish and serve:
1. Re-heat the leeks, remove the bouquet garni and divide between six warmed serving bowls.
2. Garnish with the chopped herbs and the truffle butter croutons on the side.

Braised leeks with truffles, vegetables brunoise and truffle butter croutons

# Simple carrot salad with organic bacon, cashews, honey and sherry vinegar

Organically grown or freshly dug home-grown carrots are a world apart from mass produced, fertiliser treated carrots; they are much more flavoursome, nutritious and sweet. Just combine ribbons of lightly steamed carrot with strips of smoky bacon, crunchy cashews and a vibrant dressing and you will have a fantastic starter.
Serves 6

1 kg/ 2lb 2oz carrots, peeled & trimmed
6 rashers organic smoked back bacon
1 red onion, peeled & thinly sliced
100g/ 3 ½ oz cashew nuts, toasted
2 tbsp chopped fresh herbs
1 tbsp organic clear honey
2 tbsp sherry vinegar
2 tsp wholegrain mustard
4 tbsp extra virgin olive oil

Sea salt & black pepper

1.  Peel the carrot into ribbons and briefly steam. *Refresh* in iced water and drain.
2.  Cut the bacon into 1cm/ ½″ strips and dry-fry in a frying pan until crispy. Drain on kitchen paper and reserve.
3.  To prepare the dressing, whisk together the honey, vinegar, mustard and olive oil. Season.
4.  To serve, combine the carrots with the bacon, onion and cashews. Toss with the dressing and add the herbs.
5.  Transfer to six small serving bowls and serve with crusty bread or soda bread.

# Warm salad of spiced and roasted vegetables with Wensleydale and toasted peanuts

This is a great starter that combines different textures, sweet and sour flavouring and rich winter colours. You can use one or two types of vegetable or a whole multitude. The cinnamon, cumin seeds and nutmeg create a pleasant warming taste and marry well with the natural sweetness of the roasted vegetables. I like to use a traditional hand-made organic Wensleydale cheese that just crumbles into the dish, but Stilton or Lincolnshire Poacher would work just as well.

Serves 6

Salad ingredients:
3 large carrots
2 large parsnips
½ swede
18 small button onions/shallots
½ large butternut squash
2 Chioggia Pink beetroots, or similar
½ tsp grated nutmeg
½ tsp cumin seeds
½ tsp ground cinnamon
2 tbsp groundnut oil
50g/ 2oz melted butter
2 tbsp clear wild flower honey

350g/ 12oz Wensleydale cheese, roughly cubed
2 tbsp parsley, roughly chopped
3 tbsp toasted peanuts
Sea salt & black pepper

Vinaigrette:
1 tsp Dijon mustard
1 tsp wholegrain mustard
½ garlic clove, peeled & finely crushed
25ml/ 1fl oz balsamic vinegar
2 tsp clear wild flower honey
2 tsp Worcestershire sauce
100ml/ 3 ½ fl oz groundnut oil
1 red onion, peeled & finely chopped
1 tbsp baby capers

To prepare the salad ingredients:

Pre-heat the oven to 200°C/ 400°F/ Gas mark 6.

1. Wash, peel and cut the vegetables into rough 3cm/ 1 ¼″ cubes.
2. Peel the onions and combine with the vegetables in a deep roasting tray.
3. Add the cinnamon, nutmeg, cumin, honey, oil and melted butter to the vegetables and mix well. Season and transfer to the oven and roast for 30-40 minutes until the vegetables are cooked and lightly caramelised.

Meanwhile, prepare the vinaigrette:

1. Whisk together the mustards, garlic, balsamic vinegar, honey and Worcestershire sauce in a bowl.
2. Gradually whisk in the groundnut oil and then stir in the red onion and capers. Season and reserve.

To finish and serve:

1. On six warmed serving plates, divide and arrange the roasted vegetables.
2. Spoon the cheese onto the vegetables and sprinkle with the parsley and toasted peanuts.
3. Drizzle with the vinaigrette and serve.

# Parsnip rosti with organic smoked bacon, thyme and horseradish crème fraîche

Rosti is a Swiss inspired dish usually made with potato. Here I have proposed a parsnip rosti with pieces of smoky bacon and lots of fresh thyme. The result will be a golden, crisp and slightly sweet rosti that would benefit from some hot horseradish crème fraîche and perhaps a little green salad. You will need some small pans that are 10-12cm/ 3-4″ in diameter.
Serves 6

750g parsnips, peeled & trimmed
6 rashers organic smoked back bacon
1 tbsp thyme leaves
1 free-range organic egg
1 free-range organic egg yolk

6 tbsp crème fraîche
1 tbsp hot horseradish sauce

Sea salt & black pepper
3 tbsp vegetable oil
25g/ 1oz unsalted butter

Mixed salad (page 32)

1.  Remove any woody core from the parsnips and coarsely grate them into a bowl.
2.  Cut the bacon into 1cm/ ½″ dice and dry-fry until crispy. Drain on kitchen paper and then add to the parsnips.
3.  Mix in the thyme, whole egg and egg yolk and season well.
4.  Heat a little oil and butter in each pan and divide the grated parsnip between them.
5.  Cook for 3-4 minutes over a medium heat until the base has taken on a light golden colour.
6.  Turn the rosti over and cook for a further 3-4 minutes.
7.  Remove and keep warm under tin foil.
8.  Meanwhile, combine the horseradish and crème fraîche then season.
9.  To serve, arrange the rosti on six serving plates and garnish with the crème fraîche and a little salad.

# Rabbit, Savoy cabbage and Pink Fir Apple potato terrine with sweet and sour chicory

A terrine such as this is best prepared 2 or 3 days before you plan to eat it. This gives it time to mature in flavour and for the ingredients to gel together. I believe this would make a great starter for an elegant dinner party or as a centrepiece for a lunch. You could present the terrine as a whole, perhaps decorated with various vegetables, pickles and chutneys. A 1kg/ 2lb 2oz loaf tin or terrine mould is required here. If you don't have this particular potato then Anya or Charlotte potatoes will suffice. I suggest you read through the recipe several times before commencing.
Serves 8-10

For the terrine:
2 skinned rabbits, each weighing about 450g/ 1lb
1 large onion, finely shredded
1 garlic clove, peeled & crushed
6 green Savoy cabbage leaves, washed & shredded
450g/ 1lb Pink Fir Apple potatoes, boiled & peeled
1 tbsp thyme leaves
2 tsp wholegrain mustard
2 tbsp groundnut oil
25g/ 1oz unsalted butter
100ml/ 3 ½ fl oz white wine
500ml/ 18fl oz chicken stock
10 gelatine leaves, soaked in cold water until soft
250g/ 9oz Prosciutto or Serrano ham, thinly sliced

Fresh herbs to garnish
Soda bread to serve
Extra virgin olive oil

Sea salt & black pepper

For the chicory:
6 heads red & white chicory
1 garlic clove, peeled & crushed
3 tbsp groundnut oil
1 tsp mixed spice
1 tbsp demerara sugar
50ml/ 2fl oz cider vinegar
50ml/ 2fl oz vegetable stock

*Chefs tip*
*If you would like to prepare this terrine without the rabbit, I suggest replacing it with 450g/1lb of free-range chicken breast.*

To prepare the terrine (2 to 3 days in advance):
1. Joint the rabbit (fig.1); remove the back legs (fig.2); separate the thigh from the leg (fig.3); remove the front legs (fig.4) remove the loins by cutting down each side of the back bone (fig.5); remove the mini fillets running along the underside of the backbone (fig.6); carefully extract the kidneys and liver (fig.7).
2. Cut the meat away from the leg and thigh bones (fig.8) and cut off any excess fat or sinew. Cut the leg and thigh meat into rough 2cm/ ¾″ cubes. Cut away any sinew from the loins (fig.9), but leave them whole. Chop the mini fillets coarsely. Slice the kidneys in half and remove any sinew or fat and chop coarsely. Remove any sinew or fat from the liver and chop coarsely. The rabbit is now ready for cooking (fig.10).

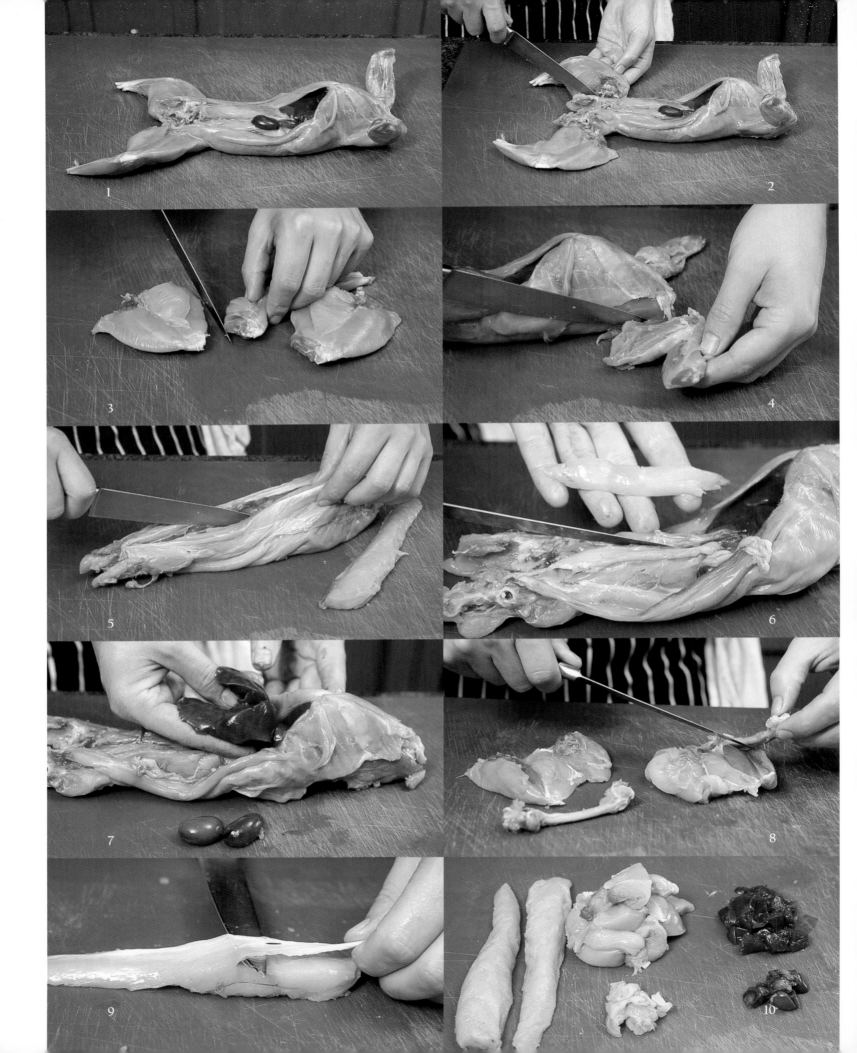

3.  Heat the groundnut oil in a large frying pan and *sweat* the onions and garlic for 2 minutes. Increase the heat; add the leg and thigh meat and *sauté* for 5 minutes.
4.  Add the white wine, thyme leaves and mustard and simmer for 3 minutes. Season, remove from the heat and then chill.
5.  In a clean frying pan, heat the unsalted butter until lightly coloured. Season the rabbit loins and sauté for 3-4 minutes turning regularly to colour evenly. Once the loins are cooked, remove from the pan and add the liver and kidneys to pan. Sauté for 30 seconds and then remove from the pan and chill.
6.  Bring a saucepan of salted water to the boil and *blanch* the shredded cabbage for 2 minutes or until just tender. *Refresh* in iced water until cold and then drain and pat dry.
7.  Line your terrine mould/loaf tin with two layers of Clingfilm and then line the two longest sides and base of the tin with the slices of ham. Leave some ham overhanging the edges as this will cover the top later.
8.  Boil 150ml/ ¼ pint of the chicken stock. Drain the soaked gelatine and melt into the stock, then combine with the remaining stock. Season and reserve.
9.  Slice the cooked potatoes into long 1cm/ ½″ thick slices. Season well.
10. **Assemble the terrine:** begin by pressing half of the leg and thigh mixture into the base of the mould. Arrange half of the sliced potatoes on the rabbit and onions. Press half of the cabbage onto the potatoes and then lay the four rabbit loins onto the meat and sprinkle the sautéed kidney, liver and mini fillets over the loins. Press the remaining cabbage onto the rabbit and then arrange the other potato slices. Finish by pressing the remaining leg and thigh mixture onto the potatoes. Try to picture the finished result when you are assembling the terrine. Each slice should have an equal quantity of rabbit, potatoes and cabbage and should look attractively arranged.
11. Pour enough stock into the mould to just cover the ingredients, making sure it is evenly distributed. Wrap the overhanging ham slices over the top of the terrine and press into place. Wrap in Clingfilm.
12. Refrigerate until the liquid has set. Place a weight (bags of sugar or flour) on the terrine and return to the fridge until required. The weight helps the terrine to set and gel together.

To prepare the chicory:
1.  Remove a little of the root base from the chicory, wash well and slice coarsely.
2.  Heat the oil in a deep frying pan and add the garlic. Sweat for 30 seconds and then add the chicory. Sauté for 2 minutes until it begins to soften.
3.  Add the demerara sugar and the mixed spice then sauté for a further minute.
4.  Pour in the cider vinegar and *deglaze* for 30 seconds over a high heat.
5.  Add the vegetable stock, *reduce* the liquid quantity by half then season well. Remove from the pan and chill until required.

To serve:
1.  Remove the terrine from the fridge 30 minutes before you intend to serve it.
2.  De-mould the terrine onto a chopping board, leaving the Clingfilm in place around the terrine. Using a sharp serrated knife, carefully slice into 2cm/ ¾″ thick slices.
3.  Remove the Clingfilm from each slice and lay the slices on a tray. Leave to rest for 20 minutes in order to take the chill off the terrine.
4.  Brush the slices with a little extra virgin olive oil and transfer to the serving plates.
5.  Spoon some sweet and sour chicory next to the terrine and garnish with the fresh herbs.
6.  Sprinkle the rabbit with a little sea salt and serve with some toasted soda bread.

Rabbit, Savoy cabbage and Pink Fir Apple potato terrine with sweet and sour chicory

# Sprouting broccoli and gorgonzola tart with toasted walnuts and wholegrain mustard dressing

This is a quick and easy dish for you to prepare and shop bought puff pastry will suffice for this recipe. I cook the pastry between two baking sheets to obtain a nice crisp and slightly caramelised base for the tart. This would make an excellent winter lunch dish to follow some home-made soup.
Serves 6

For the broccoli tart:
450g/ 1lb puff pastry (see basics)
50g/ 2oz unsalted butter, melted
300g/ 10oz Gorgonzola  cheese
6 rashers organic streaky bacon
350g/ 12oz purple sprouting broccoli
1 tbsp extra virgin olive oil

For the garnishes:
150g/ 5oz toasted walnut pieces
1 tbsp wholegrain mustard
100ml/ 3 ½ fl oz extra virgin olive oil
3 tbsp balsamic vinegar
½ tsp castor sugar
2 tbsp mixed herbs, finely chopped

Sea salt & black pepper

To prepare the broccoli tart:
Pre-heat the oven to 200°C/ 400°F/ Gas mark 6.
1. Roll out the puff pastry to an even thickness of approximately 5mm/ ¼″ and cut into six 12cm/ 5″ circles. Chill in the fridge for 20 minutes.
2. Brush the pastry with melted butter and lay the pastry circles onto greaseproof paper on a baking sheet and then cover with greaseproof paper and another baking sheet.
3. Place an ovenproof weight on the baking sheet and bake in the oven for 10-12 minutes.
4. Remove the pastry when it is lightly golden in colour and crispy. Reserve.
5. Dry-fry the bacon until crispy and steam the sprouting broccoli until tender.
6. Crush the gorgonzola with the olive oil and season.

To prepare the garnishes:
1. Combine the mustard, oil, vinegar, sugar and herbs together and season to taste.

To finish and serve:
1. Lay the pastry circles in the centre of six warmed plates and spread the cheese over the pastry.
2. Re-heat the bacon and broccoli and arrange on top of the cheese.
3. Sprinkle the toasted walnuts over the broccoli and bacon and spoon the mustard dressing around the tart. Serve.

# Steamed cod fillet with stir-fried sprouting broccoli in sesame oil, tamarind dressing

This is an easy main course to prepare and perfect for when you are short of time and want a healthy meal. Sprouting broccoli is very fashionable at the moment, which is great because it is an excellent source of Vitamin B and D and is also a low GI food.
Serves 6

6 x 250g/ 9oz thick pieces of cod fillet, skinless & boneless
1lt/ 1 ¾ pints vegetable stock (see basics)
450g/ 1lb sprouting broccoli, washed & trimmed into small florets & stems
1 garlic clove, peeled & finely crushed
3 tbsp toasted sesame seed oil
2 tbsp unsalted cashew nuts, lightly crushed
1 tbsp coriander leaves, chopped
1 long red fresh chilli, deseeded & thinly sliced

For the dressing:
1 tbsp tamarind extract
1 tsp palm sugar
Juice of 1 lime
½ tsp fish sauce
1 shallot
½ garlic clove, peeled

Sea salt & black pepper

You should prepare all of the ingredients before you begin, and then cook each element of the dish concurrently.

1. Bring the stock to the boil in a steamer. Season the cod and then steam for 8-10 minutes until firm but still translucent in appearance.
2. Heat the sesame oil in a wok and fry the garlic and chilli.
3. Add the broccoli and stir-fry for 4-5 minutes. Add a splash of water, and season and cook a little more until the broccoli is tender, but its texture and colour are retained. Finish with the cashew nuts.
4. Combine all of the dressing ingredients in a blender and puree until smooth. Check the seasoning.
5. In six warmed serving bowls, arrange the cod on a pile of the sprouting broccoli and spoon the tamarind dressing around. Serve.

# Fillet of wild sea bass with purple potato scales, steamed greens and lemongrass sauce

This is an ideal dish for the purple potato. Arranged in a scale pattern on the fish, the potatoes crisp up beautifully and provide a vivid colour contrast with the white fish. The steamed greens are kept slightly crunchy which helps them retain more of their nutritional content. I have suggested a lemongrass infused sauce that gives a nice oriental kick to the dish. Be sure to buy wild sea bass and not the intensely farmed tasteless sea bass which are flooding the market.
Serves 6

For the sea bass and potato scales:
1 whole wild sea bass, weighing about 2kg/4 ¼ lb
(Gutted, cleaned & washed)
350g/ 12oz purple potatoes, washed
75g/ 2 ½ oz unsalted butter
2 tsp arrowroot
2 tbsp olive oil
25g/ 1oz unsalted butter

For the greens:
150g/ 5oz greens
150g/ 5oz green cabbage
150g/ 5oz green curly kale

For the lemongrass sauce:
1 small onion, peeled & finely chopped
½ garlic clove, peeled & crushed
2 sticks lemongrass, crushed & chopped
200ml/ 7fl oz white wine
500ml/ 18 fl oz vegetable stock (see basics)
100ml/ 3 ½ fl oz double cream
1 bayleaf
25g/ 1oz unsalted butter

Sea salt & black pepper

To prepare the sea bass and potato scales:
1.  Remove the fillets from the sea bass and then remove the skin. If you are unsure of how to do this then ask your fishmonger to prepare it for you.
2.  Remove the bones that run along the centre of each fillet.
3.  Trim the fillets and divide into six equal pieces. Chill.
4.  Cut the potatoes into 2mm slices. Using an apple corer, cut out small circles from the potato slices.
5.  Bring a saucepan of salted water to the boil and cook the potato circles for 2-3 minutes. It is important not to overcook them at this stage.
6.  Drain the potatoes. In a separate frying pan, heat the butter and add the potatoes. Coat thoroughly in the butter and season. Remove from the heat.
7.  Mix the arrowroot with a little cold water and add to the potatoes, coating evenly.
8.  Leave the scales to cool a little and then layer them on the bass fillets in a neat overlapping scale pattern. Refrigerate until required.

To prepare the lemongrass sauce:
1. In a saucepan, add the wine, onion, garlic and lemongrass. Boil to *reduce* by half.
2. Next, add the vegetable stock and bayleaf and simmer for 10 minutes.
3. Finally, add the cream and simmer for 3 minutes. Remove from the heat, season and leave to *infuse* for 10 minutes. Liquidise and pass through a fine sieve.

To prepare the greens
1. Prepare a steamer.
2. Wash, trim and shred the mixed greens.

To finish and serve:
Pre-heat the oven to 190°C/ 375°F/ Gas mark 5.
1. Heat the olive oil and butter in a frying pan and carefully place the fish, scale side down, into the pan. Cook carefully for 5-6 minutes, until the scales are lightly golden. Turn the fish over and onto a baking tray. Place in the oven for 5-6 minutes.
2. Meanwhile, steam the mixed greens until just tender and then season.
3. Re-heat the sauce in a saucepan. Add the unsalted butter and froth with a hand blender.
4. Spoon the greens onto six serving plates and place the fish on top.
5. Spoon the frothy sauce around the fish and serve.

# Roast loin of venison with a compote of green cabbage, salsify cooked in olive oil and red wine sauce

This is a dish I prepared regularly during my days as a chef in restaurants and hotels. I like to marinate the venison overnight in groundnut oil with a few herbs and spices, which helps to tenderise the meat.
Serves 6

For the compote of green cabbage:
2 red onions, peeled & finely sliced
1 Savoy cabbage, trimmed & shredded
1 garlic clove, peeled & finely crushed
4 tbsp olive oil
4 rashers streaky bacon, finely sliced
200ml/ 7fl oz vegetable stock (see basics)
2 tsp chopped thyme & rosemary leaves
Pinch of freshly grated nutmeg

For the salsify:
6-10 sticks salsify, washed very well
500ml/ 18 fl oz olive oil
1 tsp coriander seeds
2 cardamom pods

Sea salt & black pepper

For the red wine sauce:
1 medium onion, peeled & chopped
2 carrots, peeled & chopped
1 leek, washed & chopped
2 garlic cloves, crushed
1 tbsp vegetable oil
1 bottle red wine
1lt/ 1 ¾ pints beef stock (see basics)
10 juniper berries

For the venison:
Approx 1kg/ 2lb 2oz venison loin
100ml/ 3 ½ fl oz groundnut oil
1 tbsp mixed chopped herbs
5 crushed juniper berries

To prepare the venison:
1. Trim any excess sinew from the venison and cut into six equal pieces. Combine with the oil, herbs and juniper berries and leave to *marinate* overnight.

To prepare the red wine sauce:
1. Heat the vegetable oil in a saucepan and add the onion, carrot, leek and garlic. *Sauté* until well coloured and then add the juniper berries and red wine. Bring to the boil and *reduce* by half.
2. Add the beef stock, bring to the boil and simmer until reduced by a further three quarters. *Skim* if necessary during this process. Pass through a fine sieve and reserve.

To prepare the salsify:
1. Bring a saucepan of salted water to the boil.
2. Peel then top and tail the salsify. Cut into equal sized batons about 7cm/ 2 ¾″ long and *blanch* in the boiling water for 1 minute. *Refresh* in iced water, drain and pat dry.
3. Place in a saucepan with the olive oil and spices and bring to a temperature of about 75°C/ 160°F. Use a sugar thermometer to check the temperature.
4. Cook very gently for 2 hours and then leave to cool a little in the oil.

To prepare the green cabbage compote:
1.  Heat the olive oil in a large deep frying pan and sauté the onion, garlic and bacon.
2.  Add the cabbage and cook until just beginning to soften.
3.  Add the vegetable stock, herbs and nutmeg and cook until the cabbage is just tender. Season and reserve.

To finish and serve:
Pre-heat the oven to 200°C/ 400°F/ Gas mark 6.
1.  Heat an ovenproof frying pan until very hot.
2.  Season the venison loins and seal in the hot pan on all sides. Transfer to the oven for 2 (rare) to 10 (well done) minutes. Remove and *rest* for at least 8 minutes.
3.  Re-heat the sauce, cabbage and salsify.
4.  Arrange a neat pile of cabbage in the centre of six warmed serving plates and place some salsify batons around the cabbage.
5.  Slice the venison thinly and lay across the cabbage. Pour the sauce around and serve.

# Mashed leek flan with toasted pine nuts, crisped and creamed onions

Leeks are easy to grow, hardy and one of the last vegetables to be harvested in a kitchen garden. I have suggested some goats' cheese which provides a good contrast in taste with the leeks. You could of course, substitute it for a creamy cows' cheese or a light blue cheese. A smoked cheese would also work really well in this recipe. Six round 12cm x 2 ½ cm/ 4" x 1" deep individual flan cases are needed here.
Serves 6

For the flan:
350g/ 12oz organic plain flour
175g/ 6oz unsalted butter
2 tsp sage leaves, finely chopped
Pinch of salt
1 free-range organic egg
Vegetable oil for greasing
3 large leeks, thoroughly washed & trimmed
1 tbsp extra virgin olive oil
1 tbsp crème fraîche
1 tbsp snipped chives
200g/ 7oz firm goat's cheese (matured for around 10-12 days)

For the garnishes:
4 small onions
100ml/ 3 ½ fl oz whole organic milk
100g/ 3 ½ oz organic plain flour, seasoned with salt & pepper
1lt/ 1 ¾ pints vegetable oil for deep frying
100g/ 3 ½ oz organic pine nuts, toasted
Snipped chives to garnish

Sea salt & black pepper

For the creamed onions:
2 large white onions
500ml/ 18 fl oz whole organic milk
200ml/ 7 fl oz double cream
1 garlic clove, peeled
2 cloves

To prepare the flans:
1.  Sift the flour into a bowl. Stir in the salt and sage leaves.
2.  Dice the butter and rub into the flour with your fingertips until the butter is well mixed.
3.  Add the egg and bring together until it forms a smooth dough. Wrap in Clingfilm and chill for 30 minutes.
4.  Lightly grease six small flan cases.
5.  On a lightly floured surface, divide the pastry into six, and roll out thinly into six circles big enough to fill the flan case.
6.  Line the cases with the pastry, pressing firmly into the edges. Leave any overhanging pastry to trim after cooking. Chill the cases for 20 minutes.
7.  Preheat the oven to 190°C/ 375°F/ Gas mark 5.

8. Fill the pastry cases with baking beans and '*blind bake*' in the centre of the oven for 15-20 minutes until the pastry is cooked through. Remove and carefully empty out the baking beans. Reserve.
9. Cut the leeks into 2cm/ ¾ ″ dice.
10. Bring a saucepan of salted water to the boil and cook the leeks for approximately 2 minutes. They should be *al dente*. Refresh the diced leeks in iced water, and then drain well. Reserve.

To prepare the creamed onions:
1. Peel and trim the onions and cut into quarters.
2. Place in a saucepan with the milk, cream, garlic and cloves.
3. Bring to a simmer and cook until the onions are soft.
4. Drain the onions but reserve the milk and cream. Remove the cloves. Puree the onions in a blender until smooth, adding a little milk and cream if necessary. The result should be a thick velvety puree. Season to taste and reserve.

To finish and serve:
Preheat the oven to 190°C/ 375°F/ Gas mark 5.
1. Heat the vegetable oil to 180°C/ 350°F using a sugar thermometer to check the temperature. Peel and trim the small onions and slice into circles. Separate the onion to give you onion rings.
2. Soak the onion rings in the milk and then toss them in the seasoned flour.
3. Deep-fry the onion rings in batches until crispy and then drain them on kitchen paper.
4. Reheat the leeks in a steamer for 3-4 minutes and transfer to a heatproof bowl. Add the olive oil and mash lightly with a fork. The leeks should retain some of their shape but become more homogeneous. Stir in the crème fraîche, chives and then season.
5. Divide the leeks between the pastry cases. Slice the goat's cheese and arrange it on top of the leeks. Place in the oven and cook for 5 minutes.
6. Meanwhile, reheat the creamed onions.
7. To serve, place a leek flan in the centre of the plate and top with some crispy onion rings.
8. Spoon or *quenelle* some creamed onion around the flan; sprinkle with the toasted pine nuts, chives and then serve.

**The Essence - Contemporary recipes inspired by a traditional kitchen garden**

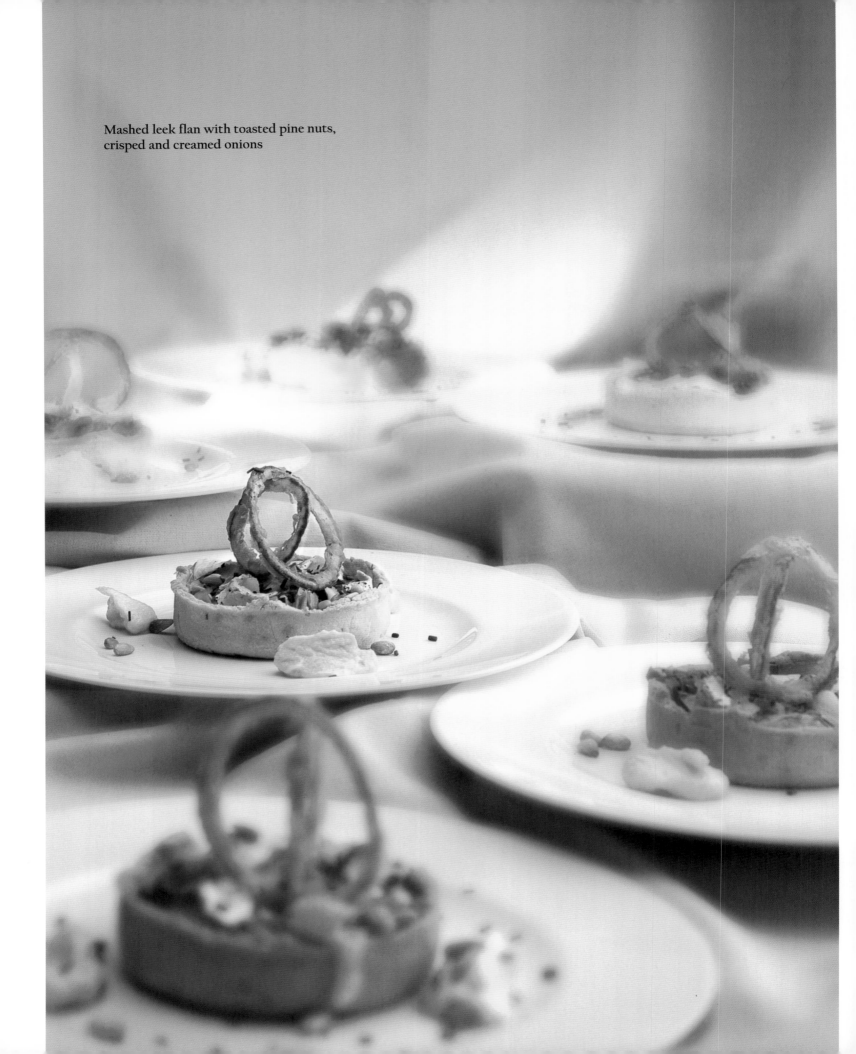

Mashed leek flan with toasted pine nuts,
crisped and creamed onions

# Winter stew of curly kale, potatoes and truffles

This is a rich earthy stew enhanced by truffles and grated Italian cheese. As you can see from the photograph, by using a variety of potatoes it becomes a visually enticing dish, which will really show off the quality of your potatoes.

Serves 6

1kg/ 2lb 2oz mixed potatoes, of similar size
350g/ 12oz mixed curly kale, washed
500ml/ 18 fl oz vegetable stock (see basics)
1 garlic clove, peeled & finely crushed
2 tsp white truffle oil
1 small truffle, thinly sliced
100g/ 3 ½ oz Parmigiano Reggiano or Gran Padano cheese

Sea salt & black pepper

*Chefs tip*
*Fresh truffles, a fruit fungus, are an exquisite luxury item. My favourite is the white truffle, whose heady aroma and taste impart a unique and distinctive flavour to a dish. The list of specialist purveyor's on page 285 may help you in sourcing fresh truffles.*

1.  Cook each variety of potatoes separately in boiling salted water until they are three quarters cooked. *Refresh* and drain them. Peel if necessary and cut into bite sized pieces.
2.  Remove any fibrous stalk from the kale, tear into pieces and *blanch* in boiling salted water for 30 seconds.
3.  Refresh in iced water and drain.
4.  Combine the garlic with the vegetable stock and add the potatoes.
5.  Return to a low heat and simmer until the potatoes are cooked through.
6.  Add the kale and simmer for a further 2 minutes.
7.  Add the truffle oil and correct the seasoning.
8.  Spoon into deep serving bowls and scatter with shavings of cheese and slices of truffle. Serve.

# Salad of lobster with chicory, blood orange and crispy chorizo

There are a real variety of flavours, textures and colours within this dish. What makes this recipe so outstanding is the combination of the spicy chorizo, bitter chicory, sweet lobster and sharp oranges. Be generous with the size of lobster you buy because it is not something eaten everyday. If you are an adventurous kitchen gardener you may well have some chicory growing in the darkest corner of your shed or cold store.
Serves 6

6 x 450g/ 1lb live lobsters
3 chicory heads, washed & trimmed
3 blood oranges, peeled & segmented
100g/ 3 ½ oz chorizo, peeled & finely sliced
1 large red onion, peeled, halved & finely sliced
1 tbsp flat-leaf parsley, washed & picked
2 tsp chives, snipped
50ml/ 2fl oz extra virgin olive oil

Sea salt & black pepper

1. Prepare the lobsters by first chilling them in iced water or the freezer to dull their senses, then plunging a large knife through the cross on the top of the head both ways.
2. Bring a large saucepan of salted water to the boil and *poach* the lobsters (two at a time) for 10 minutes. *Refresh* in iced water and repeat until all the lobsters are cooked.
3. Referring to page 119 for direction, remove the meat from the claws, knuckles and tail and reserve on a tray. (You could use the lobster heads and shells to make a lobster soup)
4. In a large bowl, combine all the ingredients together and season to taste.
5. Arrange onto six serving plates and serve.

# Spiced and glazed belly pork
# with stir-fried Brussels sprouts

This dish really encapsulates what I love about cooking and eating. The slow cooking of a piece of flavoursome meat with the addition of herbs and spices produces a wonderfully sumptuous result. The pork belly should hold its shape, but at the same time be meltingly tender.
Serves 6

For the spiced & glazed belly pork:
1.5kg/ 3 ¼ lb pork belly joint
3 tbsp vegetable oil
2 carrots, peeled & roughly chopped
1 leek, washed & roughly chopped
1 onion, peeled & roughly chopped
2 garlic cloves, roughly chopped
1 tbsp coriander seeds
1 tsp cumin seeds
½ cinnamon stick
1 star anise
3 cloves
100ml/ 3 ½ fl oz balsamic vinegar
2 lts/ 2 ½ pints beef stock (see basics)
2 tbsp clear organic honey

Sea salt & black pepper
100g/ 3 ½ oz unsalted butter

For the Brussels sprouts:
450g/ 1lb sprouts, shredded
150g/ 5oz fennel
1 red onion, peeled & thinly sliced
1 garlic clove, peeled & finely crushed
4 tbsp vegetable oil
100ml/ 3 ½ fl oz chicken stock (see basics)

*Chefs tip*
*As with all the meat you purchase, I recommend you take interest in the provenance of the product. Free-range and special-breed pork is readily available all over the country.*

To prepare the belly pork:
Pre-heat the oven to 180°C/ 350°F/ Gas mark 4.
1.  Using a sharp thin knife, cut the fat off the pork belly to an even thickness of approximately 5mm/ ¼".Cut away the rib bones and even out the overall thickness of the belly. Cut into six equal sized squares.
2.  Heat the oil in a large heavy frying pan and cook the belly pork over quite a high heat, until the pork is golden and caramelised.
3.  Remove the pork and add the vegetables and garlic to the pan. *Sauté* until well coloured and then add the spices and balsamic vinegar. Cook for a further minute.
4.  Add the beef stock, season and transfer to an ovenproof casserole dish. Cover and cook in the oven for 3 hours. The belly pork should feel tender but still be holding its shape.

5.  Leave to cool in the cooking liquid and then remove the pork. Place the pork on a tray, cover with Clingfilm and weigh it down with a heavy object. Place in the fridge and chill for 3 hours.
6.  *Skim* any fat and impurities from the cooking liquid and *reduce* by two thirds over a high heat.
7.  Pass the sauce through a fine sieve or muslin cloth and reserve.

To finish and serve:
NB: prepare all the components concurrently:
1.  Place the pork belly portions into the frying pan and add the honey with a little of the sauce. Begin to cook and caramelise over a medium heat until the pork is well glazed on either side. Remove and rest for 5 minutes before serving.
2.  Heat the vegetable oil in a wok and add the onions, fennel and garlic. Stir-fry for 1 minute and then add the sprouts. Continue to stir-fry, adding a little stock if necessary until the sprouts are just tender. Season.
3.  Re-heat the sauce and then turn the heat to very low. Gradually whisk in the butter until completely *emulsified*. Adjust the seasoning.
4.  To serve, place a bed of sprouts in the centre of six warmed serving bowls, place a belly pork portion on each and pour the sauce around.

Spiced and glazed belly
pork with stir-fried
Brussels sprouts

# Guanaja chocolate tart scented with fennel and chilli

Christopher Columbus encountered cocoa beans in Guanaja on a Mayan trading canoe during 1502 on his voyage to the New World. Guanaja chocolate is high in cocoa solids as all quality chocolate should be. Here I have continued the Aztec theme by combining chilli with chocolate. The flavour of the fennel also marries well, and the result is a chocolate tart with a spicy kick.
Serves 6-8

For the tart pastry:
200g/ 7oz plain flour
50g/ 2 oz cocoa powder
150g/ 5 oz unsalted butter
100g/ 3 ½ oz icing sugar
2 egg yolks
½ tsp fennel seeds, finely crushed
Salt

For the chocolate ganache filling:
100ml/ 3 ½ fl oz organic whole milk
75ml/ 2 ½ fl oz double cream
450g/ 1lb Guanaja 70% chocolate
1 red chilli, de-seeded
½ tsp fennel seeds, finely crushed
1 star anise, crushed
2 free-range organic eggs

For the garnishes:
200ml/ 7 fl oz double cream
2 tsp icing sugar
1 tsp vanilla extract
200g/ 7oz fresh fennel bulb
1 organic lemon
Dried flaked chilli
Cocoa powder

To prepare the pastry:
1. Sift the flour, cocoa powder and salt together.
2. Mix in the sugar. Dice the butter and rub into the flour.
3. Add the egg yolks and fennel seeds and bring together to form a smooth dough.
4. Wrap in Clingfilm and chill for 30 minutes.
5. Grease a 20cm/ 8″ tart/flan case.
6. Roll out the pastry on a lightly floured surface to an even thickness of 3-4mm/ ⅛″.
7. Line the case, pressing gently into the edges. Leave an overhang around the top edge of about 1cm/ ½″. Chill for 30 minutes.
8. Pre-heat the oven to 190°/ 375°F/ Gas mark 5.
9. Line the pastry with baking beans and '*blind bake*' in the centre of the oven for approximately 25-30 minutes. The pastry should just be starting to crisp all over and have no uncooked areas on its base. Cool and reserve.

To prepare the chocolate ganache filling:
1. Chop or break the chocolate into small pieces. Gently melt in a *Bain Marie* until the chocolate has completely melted. It should not get any hotter than blood temperature.
2. Finely chop the chilli, and bring to the boil with the milk, cream, fennel seeds and star anise.
3. Cool the cream and milk slightly, and gradually whisk into the chocolate. Leave to *infuse* for 15 minutes and then add the eggs and mix in well. Pass the chocolate through a fine sieve. This is known as ganache.
4. Pre-heat the oven to 200°C/ 400°F/ Gas mark 6.
5. Pour the chocolate ganache into the pastry case and place in the centre of the oven.
6. Turn the oven off and leave the tart for 45-60 minutes until it is just set.
7. Remove from the oven and rest at room temperature for at least 2 hours before serving.

To finish and serve:
1. Trim the pastry edges of the tart with scissors and turn out the tart.
2. Trim and peel the fennel of any woody or fibrous flesh. Cut into very thin slices.
3. Grate the zest from the lemon and extract the juice. Add to the fennel and combine with a little of the dried chilli flakes.
4. Whisk the cream with the icing sugar and vanilla.
5. Slice the tart and serve garnished with the fennel and whipped cream.
6. Dust with cocoa powder and serve.

Valrhona chocolate and chillies

The Essence - Contemporary recipes inspired by a traditional kitchen garden        253

# Chestnut pudding with caramel pears and chestnut ice cream

This is great winter dessert that can be made in a standard 20cm/8″ cake tin, or in smaller individual moulds that may be more suited to a dinner party. Ready prepared chestnuts and chestnut puree are available for you to use, or you could prepare your own if you so desire.
Serves 6-8

For the chestnut pudding:
2 free-range organic eggs
75g/ 2 ½ oz light brown soft sugar
75g/ 2 ½ oz crushed roasted chestnuts
125g/ 4oz ground almonds

For the caramel pears:
4 small firm pears, Packham or Comice
75g/ 2 ½ oz light brown soft sugar
50g/ 2oz unsalted butter
150g/ 5oz castor sugar
100ml/ 3 ½ fl oz pure apple juice

For the chestnut ice cream:
500ml/ 18 fl oz organic milk
6 free-range organic egg yolks
100g/ 3 ½ oz castor sugar
100g/ 3 ½ oz chestnut puree

For the garnish:
100g/ 3 ½ oz crushed roasted chestnuts

To prepare the chestnut ice cream:
1. Bring the milk to the boil in a heavy based saucepan.
2. Whisk the egg yolks and sugar together in a heatproof bowl. Add the chestnut puree and mix well.
3. Pour the milk onto the eggs gradually and whisk well.
4. Return to a clean saucepan and cook over a low heat until the mixture thickens enough to coat the back of a spoon. Chill immediately over iced water.
5. Once chilled, churn in an ice cream machine and freeze until required.

To prepare the caramel pears:
1. Peel, quarter and core the pears. Heat the butter in a frying pan and cook the pears over a medium to high heat until they begin to colour. Add the brown sugar and continue to cook until the pears caramelise. Remove from heat and reserve.
2. In a separate saucepan, heat the sugar over a medium heat until it has melted and then formed a light golden caramel. Remove from the heat and carefully add the apple juice.
3. Return to a medium heat and cook for a few minutes. The result should be a rich caramel sauce.
4. Add the pears; remove from the heat and leave to *infuse* at room temperature until required.

To prepare the chestnut pudding:

Pre-heat the oven to 180°C/ 350°F/ Gas mark 4.

1. Lightly butter the large cake tin or the six to eight smaller individual oven-proof moulds and place them on a baking tray.
2. Whisk the eggs and sugar together in an electric mixer until they have tripled in volume.
3. Gently fold in the almonds, chestnuts and baking powder. Transfer to the greased moulds and bake in the centre of the oven. The smaller puddings will take approximately 8-10 minutes. The larger pudding will take 20-25 minutes.
4. Remove from the oven and moulds.

To finish and serve:

1. Place the individual chestnut puddings or a slice of the whole pudding in the centre of the serving plates. Spoon four pieces of pear around the pudding and drizzle with some caramel sauce. Place a scoop of the ice cream on top of the pudding. Scatter with some roasted chestnut pieces and serve.

# My apple and cinnamon crumble with honey ice cream

Everybody has a favourite crumble recipe and this is mine. I love apples that retain their texture and are redolent of cinnamon. For the crumble topping I like a crispy but crumbly finish. Honey ice cream complements the crumble perfectly, especially if the honey is locally produced.
Serves 6-8 (individual crumbles)

For the apples:
6-8 Cox's Pomona or Braeburn apples
50g/ 2oz unsalted butter
75g/ 2 ½ oz light brown soft sugar
100ml/ 3 ½ fl oz pure apple juice
1 tsp ground cinnamon

For the crumble topping:
100g/ 3 ½ oz plain organic flour
25g/ 1oz wholemeal organic flour
100g/ 3 ½ oz unsalted butter, diced
50g/ 2 oz demerara sugar
Salt

For the honey ice cream:
500ml/ 18fl oz whole organic milk
6 free-range organic egg yolks
75g/ 2 ½ oz castor sugar
1 vanilla pod, spilt
3 tbsp clear wild flower honey

Ground cinnamon to garnish

To prepare the honey ice cream:
1.  Bring the milk with the vanilla pod to the boil.
2.  Meanwhile, whisk the egg yolks and sugar together in a heatproof bowl. Mix in the honey.
3.  Gradually pour the hot milk onto the eggs and whisk well.
4.  Return to a low heat in a clean saucepan and cook, stirring constantly, until the mixture is thick enough to coat the back of a spoon.
5.  Chill the pan immediately over iced water.
6.  Once chilled, churn in an ice cream machine and then freeze until required.

To prepare the crumble topping:
1.  Sift the flours together and add the salt.
2.  Next, add the sugar and then rub the butter into the flour and bring together to form a smooth dough.
3.  Gently roll out the pastry dough onto a lightly floured surface to an even thickness of about 5mm/ ¼".
4.  Chill the rolled out pastry dough on a baking tray.

To prepare the apples:
Pre-heat the oven to 200°C/ 400°F/ Gas mark 6.

1. Rinse, quarter and core the apples.
2. Heat the butter in a large frying pan and *sauté* the apples until lightly coloured.
3. Add the sugar and cinnamon and caramelise lightly.
4. Add the apple juice and cook for 2 minutes over a medium heat. The apples should be golden in colour, tender but still maintaining the majority of their shape.
5. Place the apples into six individual ovenproof moulds on a baking tray.
6. Take the pastry and break off thumbnail sized pieces. Arrange these pieces in an overlapping pattern over the apples.
7. Place the crumbles in the centre of the oven and cook for 20 minutes. The crumble topping should be crisp and lightly golden.
8. Remove from the moulds and transfer the crumbles to six serving plates. Spoon any resulting apple cooking juices around the crumble, dust with cinnamon and serve with a scoop or two of the ice cream.

# Caramelised apple feuilleté
# with Madagascan vanilla cream and apple compote

Crisp pastry, rich vanilla cream and the acidity from the apples provide the perfect combination for a mouth watering dessert. The choice of apple is yours, but I have successfully used Golden Noble, George Neal, Ribston Pippin, Braeburn and Cox's Pomona. If you would like to serve a dessert wine with this, then I suggest a rich Hungarian Tokaji or a Canadian Icewine. Madagascar produces fabulously plump vanilla pods that impart that unique universally loved flavour.
Serves 6

For the apple feuilleté:
450g/ 1lb puff pastry (see basics)
100g/ 3 ½ oz icing sugar
6-8 apples, peeled, quartered & cored
75g/ 2 ½ oz light brown soft sugar
Pinch of ground cinnamon
1 tsp vanilla extract

For the vanilla cream:
250ml/ 9 fl oz double cream
100ml/ 3 ½ fl oz whole organic milk
5 free-range organic egg yolks
75g/ 2 ½ oz castor sugar
1 tbsp cornflour
1 Madagascar vanilla pod, split

For the apple compote:
4-6 apples, peeled, quartered & cored
25g/ 1oz unsalted butter
50g/ 2oz light brown soft sugar

For the garnish:
50g/ 2oz toasted flaked almonds

To prepare the vanilla cream:
1. In a heavy based saucepan, bring the milk, cream and vanilla pod to the boil.
2. Meanwhile, whisk the egg yolks, castor sugar and cornflour together in a heatproof bowl.
3. Gradually pour the milk onto the eggs and mix well.
4. Return to the heat in a clean saucepan and bring back to the boil, stirring constantly.
5. Boil for 2-3 minutes, until you can no longer taste the cornflour.
6. Pass through a fine sieve.
7. Pour into a small Clingfilm lined baking tray. The vanilla cream needs to be approximately 2cm/ ¾ " thick.
8. Chill the vanilla cream until required.

To prepare the apple feuilleté:
Pre-heat the oven to 200°C/ 400°F/ Gas mark 6.
1. On a lightly floured surface, roll out the pastry to a rectangle with an even thickness of about 3-4mm/ ⅛".
2. Place on a greased baking sheet and chill for 20 minutes.
3. Cover the pastry with a sheet of greaseproof paper and then with another baking tray. Place a large, ovenproof weight on the tray and then place in the oven.
4. Cook for approximately 20 minutes. The pastry should be cooked but not risen.
5. Remove the top baking tray, the greaseproof paper and dust the pastry with the icing sugar.

6. Return to the top of the oven and cook until the icing sugar just caramelises. Remove and carefully cut the pastry into twelve equal rectangles. Reserve.
7. Cut the apples into 1cm/ ½″ thick slices and place in a large frying pan with the sugar, cinnamon and vanilla. Cook over a medium to high heat until the apples soften and take on a little colour from the sugar. Cool and reserve.

To prepare the apple compote:
1. Cut the apples into 1cm/ ½″ cubes. Melt the butter in a frying pan and fry the apples until lightly coloured. Add the sugar and cook for a further minute. Cool and reserve.

To finish and serve:
1. Remove the vanilla cream to a chopping board and cut into six rectangles the same size as the pastry.
2. On six serving plates, spoon a tiny amount of the vanilla cream trimmings onto the centre.
3. Place a rectangle of the pastry firmly on the vanilla cream.
4. Top the pastry with a rectangle of vanilla cream and then with some of the sliced apples.
5. Finish with another rectangle of the pastry. Spoon some of the apple compote around the feuilleté and sprinkle with the toasted almonds. Serve.

The Essence - Contemporary recipes inspired by a traditional kitchen garden

# Date and clove shortbread with steeped quince and lemon clotted cream

This is a simple dessert to prepare, particularly as you can make use of quinces that you may have steeped earlier in the season. As well as a dessert, this recipe may be suitable to incorporate into an afternoon tea.
Serves 6

For the shortbread:
450g/ 1lb plain organic flour
200g/ 7oz unsalted butter, diced
100g/ 3 ½ oz castor sugar
100g/ 3 ½ oz semi-dried organic dates
5 cloves, finely ground
Salt

For the clotted cream:
6 tbsp clotted cream
Zest & juice of 1 organic lemon

4 steeped quince (page 272)

To prepare the shortbread:
1. Sift the flour with a pinch of salt into a bowl. Mix the sugar into the flour and then rub in the butter.
2. Chop the dates finely and mix into the shortbread with the cloves.
3. Bring the dough together, adding a touch of water if necessary. Chill for 30 minutes before use.
4. Pre-heat the oven to 190°C/ 375°F/ Gas mark 5.
5. Gently roll out the shortbread dough on a lightly floured surface and cut out into shapes of your choice. Arrange on a greaseproof paper lined baking tray and chill for 5 minutes.
6. Bake in the centre of the oven until very lightly coloured, slightly spring to the touch and crisp on removal from the oven.

To finish and serve:
1. Cut the quince into bite sized pieces.
2. Mix the clotted cream with the lemon juice and zest. Spoon 1 tbsp of the cream onto each serving plate.
3. Arrange the quince around the plate and finish with the shortbread. Serve.

# <u>Basics</u>

## Stocks

Stocks are the backbone of the kitchen and it is nearly always necessary to have a supply of homemade stock available. Once you have prepared your different stocks I recommend that you label and freeze them in small freezer bags. Then, every time you require some stock you can just defrost the required type.

<u>Bouquet garni:</u> Essential for flavouring and seasoning stocks, soups and sauces.

2 large green ends of leek
½ stick celery
2 bay leaves
3 sprigs parsley
2 sprigs thyme
6 black peppercorns

Wrap the celery, bay leaves, parsley, thyme and peppercorns in the separated leek leaves and tie together with string.

Vegetable stock: (makes about 2 ½ litres/3 ½ pints)

2 large onions
2 garlic cloves
4 carrots
2 leeks
3 sticks celery
1 bouquet garni
2 tbsp vegetable oil
3 lts/ 5 ¼ pints water

1. Wash, peel and roughly chop the vegetables.
2. Heat the oil in a large saucepan and fry the vegetables until lightly coloured.
3. Add the water and bouquet garni.
4. Bring to the boil, *skim* and simmer for 1 hour.
5. Strain through a fine sieve and cool.

Chicken stock: (makes about 3 litres/ 5 ¼ pints)

2 chicken carcasses
2 large onions
2 garlic cloves
2 carrots
1 leek
2 sticks celery
1 bouquet garni
2 tbsp vegetable oil
4 lts/ 6 pints of cold water

1. Preheat the oven to 240°C/ 475°F/ Gas mark 8.
2. Trim the chicken carcasses of any fat and cut into apple-sized chunks.
3. Roast in the oven until golden brown. Drain the chicken on kitchen paper.
4. Wash, peel and roughly chop the vegetables.
5. Heat the oil in a large saucepan and fry the vegetables until golden.
6. Add the roasted chicken, water and bouquet garni.
7. Bring to the boil, *skim* and simmer for 2 ½ hours, skimming occasionally.
8. Strain through a fine sieve and cool.

<u>Beef/Veal stock</u>: (makes about 3 litres/ 5 ¼ pints)

1 ½ kg/ 3lb small beef or veal bones
2 large onions
2 garlic cloves
2 carrots
1 leek
2 sticks celery
1 bouquet garni
1 tbsp tomato puree
2 tbsp vegetable oil
5 lts/ 7 ¾ pints of cold water

1.   Preheat the oven to 250°C/ 500°F/ Gas mark 9.
2.   Roast the bones in the oven until well browned. Drain the bones on kitchen paper.
3.   Wash, peel and roughly chop the vegetables.
4.   Heat the oil in a large saucepan and fry the vegetables until well coloured.
5.   Add the bones, bouquet garni, tomato puree and water.
6.   Bring to the boil, *skim* and simmer for 3 ½ hours, skimming occasionally.
7.   Strain through a fine sieve and cool.

**Stock making**

# Vinegar, oil and egg based dressings

These are required throughout this book for a number of recipes. The vinaigrettes always make a good accompaniment for salads and vegetables, whilst the flavoured oils add a unique aspect and colour to a variety of recipes.

## Basic vinaigrette:

50ml/ 2 fl oz white wine vinegar
Pinch of salt
Black pepper
1 tsp wholegrain mustard
2 tsp lemon juice
150ml/ 5 fl oz extra virgin olive oil

1. Whisk the vinegar, salt, pepper, mustard and lemon juice together.
2. Gradually whisk in the olive oil.
3. Check the seasoning.

## Balsamic vinaigrette:

50ml/ 2 fl oz balsamic vinegar
1 tsp Dijon mustard
Pinch of salt
Black pepper
2 tsp lemon juice
150ml/ 5 fl oz extra virgin olive oil

Follow the same method as for the basic vinaigrette.

## Shallot vinaigrette:

50ml/ 2 fl oz red wine vinegar
1 tsp wholegrain mustard
2 small shallots, peeled & very finely diced
Pinch of salt
Black pepper
2 tsp lemon juice
150ml/ 5 fl oz extra virgin olive oil

1. Whisk together the red wine vinegar, mustard, salt, pepper and lemon juice.
2. Whisk in the shallots.
3. Gradually whisk in the olive oil.
4. Check the seasoning

Herb oil:

150g/ 5oz mixed picked herbs (basil, chives, parsley, coriander, chervil)
300ml/ 10 fl oz vegetable oil
Salt & black pepper

1. Wash and thoroughly dry the herbs.
2. Puree in a blender with the oil.
3. Season to taste and pass through a fine sieve.
4. Refrigerate for up to 10 days.

Cèpe oil:

100g/ 3 ½ oz fresh cèpe trimmings or dried cèpes (soaked first in cold water)
300ml/ 10fl oz vegetable oil
Sea salt & black pepper

1. Clean the cèpes and thoroughly dry on kitchen paper.
2. Take 1 tbsp of the oil and heat in a frying pan.
3. Sauté the cèpes until golden brown.
4. Add to the oil and puree in a blender.
5. Season and pass through a fine sieve.
6. Refrigerate for up to 10 days.

Mustard oil:

300ml/ 10fl oz vegetable oil
2 tsp English mustard
Salt and pepper
1 tsp castor sugar
2 tbsp wholegrain mustard
Sea salt & black pepper

1. Whisk the oil, English mustard and seasonings and sugar together.
2. Whisk in the wholegrain mustard.
3. Check the seasoning.
4. Refrigerate for up to 3 weeks.

Chilli oil:

300ml/ 10 fl oz vegetable oil
3 red chillies
3 green chillies
1 tsp coriander seeds, toasted
1 tsp cumin seeds, toasted
Sea salt & black pepper

1. Split the chillies in half and combine with the other ingredients in a kilner jar or bottle. Leave to infuse for a minimum of 1 week before use. This will keep in the fridge for at least 3 months.

The Essence - Contemporary recipes inspired by a traditional kitchen garden          267

<u>Tarragon vinegar:</u>

1lt/1 ¾ pints white wine vinegar
150g/ 5oz fresh tarragon, washed & dried

1.  Simply combine the two ingredients in a kilner jar or bottle and leave to *infuse* for a minimum of 1 week before use. This will keep for at least 3 months.

<u>Mint vinegar:</u>

1lt/ 1 ¾ pints white wine vinegar
150g/ 5oz fresh mint, washed & dried

1.  Simply combine the two ingredients in a kilner jar or bottle and leave to *infuse* for a minimum 1 week before use. This will keep for at least 3 months.

# Pastry goods

Below are a few basic recipes for different types of pastry products. Be sure to read through the recipes first as some recipes require more time than you may think.

<u>Puff pastry:</u>

This recipe is credited to Jean Millet, a legendary French pâtisser. The recipe can be found in "The Roux Brothers on Patisserie", published by Little, Brown. One of my most vivid memories of making puff pastry was during my time working in Paris. I remember being sent to the cold basement with a 25kg batch of puff pastry to turn. After many hours the Head Pastry Chef was finally happy with the result. I can assure you that making puff pastry is not actually that difficult - it just requires more time than other pastries.

500g/ 17oz plain flour, plus a little extra for rolling & turning
200ml/ 7fl oz water
12g/ ⅓ oz salt
25ml/ 1 fl oz white wine vinegar
50g/ 2oz butter, melted
400g/ 13oz butter, well chilled

For the dough:
1.  Place the flour on a work surface and make a well in the centre. Pour in the water, salt, vinegar and melted butter. Work together with your fingertips and gradually draw in the flour and mix well.
2.  Once all the ingredients are well mixed, work the dough with the palm of your hand until it is completely homogeneous. Roll into a ball and cut a cross in the top to break the elasticity. Wrap in Clingfilm and refrigerate for 2-3 hours.

Incorporating the butter:
1. Lightly flour the work surface. Roll the ball of dough in four different places so it looks like four large ears around a small round head (Fig.1).
2. Hit the chilled butter pastry several times with a rolling pin so that it is supple but still firm and very cold.
3. Place the butter on the head of the pastry so that it covers it but does not overhang (Fig.2).
4. Fold the ears over the butter to cover it completely (Fig.3). Chill in the fridge for 30 minutes to bring the butter and dough to the same temperature.

Turning and folding the pastry:
1. Lightly flour the work surface, and then progressively roll the dough away from you into a rectangle of about 70 x 40cm/ 30x15″ (Fig.4). Fold over the ends to make three layers (Fig.5). This is the first turn.
2. Repeat this process and then chill in the fridge for 30 minutes.
3. Make four more turns, chilling after two turns.

The pastry is now ready to use. It will keep for 3 days in the fridge or for up to 3 weeks in the freezer.

Puff pastry preparation

The Essence - Contemporary recipes inspired by a traditional kitchen garden

<u>Sweet pastry</u>: (enough to line a 20cm/ 8″ flan case)

350g/ 12oz plain flour, sifted
115g/ 3 ¾ oz icing sugar
160g/ 5 ½ oz soft unsalted butter, diced
Seeds of 1 vanilla pod
1 egg
Pinch of salt

1. Combine the flour, salt, icing sugar and vanilla pod seeds together.
2. Add the butter and mix in using your fingertips.
3. When the butter is well mixed into the flour, add the egg and mix to a smooth dough.
4. Refrigerate for 30 minutes before use.


<u>Short savoury pastry</u> :( enough to line a 20cm/ 8″ flan case)

350g/ 12oz plain flour, sifted
175g/ 6oz unsalted butter, diced
Pinch of salt
1 tsp dried mixed herbs
1 egg

1. Combine the flour, salt and herbs together.
2. Mix in the butter using your fingertips until well mixed.
3. Add the egg and bring together to form a smooth dough.
4. Refrigerate for at least 30 minutes before use.


# Breadcrumbs

When dried breadcrumbs are required I prefer to use Panko breadcrumbs which are readily available in Oriental supermarkets. However, breadcrumbs are easy to make yourself. Simply dry out white or wholemeal slices of bread in a low temperature oven until they are crispy. Next, transfer to a food processor and blend until you are left with fine even breadcrumbs. As a variation, you could add dried herbs such as rosemary or thyme, some dried chilli flakes or even freshly grated lemon zest.

# Steeped fruits and compotes

These are fantastic as accompaniments to desserts as well as breakfast dishes in their own right.

Dried fruit compote:

1kg/2lb 2oz mixed dried fruits (prunes, figs, mango, apricots, and apple)
250g/ 9oz mixed organic nuts (pecans, Brazils, walnuts)
2 cinnamon sticks
2 star anise
1 vanilla pod, split
5 cloves
2 fruit tea bags
1 orange, sliced

1. Place the fruits and nuts in a heatproof bowl and add the spices, teabags and orange slices. Cover with boiling water.
2. Press the fruits to ensure they are all covered in water/juice and leave to cool.
3. Once cold, refrigerate and leave to *steep* for at least 1 week before use. Remove the tea bags before eating. This should keep for up to 1 month in the fridge.

Steeped quince:

4 large quince, peeled, quartered & cored
100g/ 3 ½ oz demerara sugar
1 cinnamon stick
1 star anise
5 cloves
1 vanilla pod
5 cardamoms
1 lemon, sliced
1lt/ 1 ¾ pints water

1. Combine the ingredients in a saucepan and bring to a gentle simmer.
2. Cover and cook gently until the quince is just cooked through.
3. Remove from the heat and allow to cool.
4. Transfer to a sealed container and refrigerate for up to 1 month.

# Seasonal menus and wine suggestions

In this section, I have listed some seasonal menu suggestions for dinner parties. The majority of the dishes can be found in the book, whilst the others should be achievable by the keen home cook, especially after having prepared some of the recipes included here. When I devise dinner party menus, I like to offer guests a wide variety of seasonal produce but in manageable portion sizes. The menus include as many as five or six courses, of which three will be of "taster" size. I have also suggested styles of wine to accompany and complement the menus.

## 'Spring menu one'

Taster of broad bean soup with herb oil
(Pages 31 & 266)

~

New season garden vegetables with Old Cotswold Legbar egg and Jabugo ham
(Page 25)
*Alan Scott Marlborough Sauvignon Blanc (latest vintage), New Zealand*
*This is unoaked wine is fresh and exuberant and perfect for celebrating the arrival of spring*

~

Herb roasted fillet of beef with wild garlic, Morels and crispy new season potatoes
(Page 60)
*Morellino di Scansano, Santa Maria Estate, Maremma, Italy*
*A rich Sangiovese full of dark berry and truffle aromas*

~

Taster of fresh gooseberry juice

~

White chocolate parfait with strawberry compote and crisps
(Page 77)
*Banyuls, M. Chapoutier, South of France*
*This is a fortified Grenache that is rich, sweet and voluptuous*

## 'Spring menu two'

Taster of asparagus soup with chive crème fraîche

-

Aromatic duck salad with marinated young beetroots
(Page 45)
*Hamilton Russell Chardonnay, South Africa*
*A lightly oaked chardonnay with crisp, citrus nutty notes*

-

Wild sea trout and shrimps baked in a paper parcel
with broad beans and marjoram, broad bean sauce
(Page 50)
*Sancerre Rose (latest vintage)*
*Pinot noir rose with a delicate salmon colour and notes of crisp summer fruit*

-

Miniature strawberry and lavender jelly
(taken from page 74, and served in a shot glass)

-

Rhubarb and blood orange tart with vanilla ice cream and cinnamon butterscotch
(taken from page 82)
*Tokaji Aszu 5 Puttonyos, Hungary*
*The Tokaji Aszu is an intense wine with honey and mango flavours*

## 'Summer menu one'

Simple summer gazpacho soup
(page 94, served in a coffee cup)

~

Grilled red mullet with saffron and crunchy fennel salad
(page 111)
*Albarino Pazo de Barrantes, Rias Baixas, Spain*
*This Albarino displays notes of lemon, apple and grapefruit*

~

Rump of Yorkshire spring lamb with caramelised onion tart,
pea and chorizo salad and goat's cheese
(page 125)
*Chateau Leoville Barton, St. Julien, Bordeaux*
*A great quality cabernet/merlot full of black fruit, chestnut and truffle aromas*

~

Miniature raspberry and Pimm's jelly with cucumber and mint compote
(taken from page 134, served in a shot glass)

~

Pistachio panna cotta with warm cherries and lavender
(page 145)
*Nivole D'Asti, Piemonte, Italy*
*A lightly sparkling Moscato which is very grapey, delicate and refreshing*

## 'Summer menu two'

Taster of chilled courgette and avocado soup
(page 110, served in a coffee cup)

-

Warm salad of new season potatoes with dwarf beans and crispy ham
(page 105)
*Pouilly Fume Chateau de Tracy, Loire*
*An unoaked herbaceous Sauvignon Blanc with notes of asparagus and peaches*

-

John Dory steamed with herbs, served with stuffed baby tomatoes and rocket sauce
(page 116, served as a half portion)

-

Poached lobster with baby spinach and chard, orange zest and sherry vinegar butter sauce
(page 119)
*Puligny Montrachet Premier Cru (3-5 years old)*
*A unoaked nutty Chardonnay with lemon and lime flavours*

-

Simple salad of strawberries, raspberries and redcurrants sprinkled with mint and rose water
*Taittinger Brut Prestige Rosé*
*This is a Pinot Noir dominated rosé champagne with flavours of refreshing red fruit*

## 'Autumn menu one'

Purple potato crisps with truffle mayonnaise
(page 162, served as an appetiser)

-

Roasted pumpkin salad with organic feta cheese and pickled walnuts
(page 167, serve as a half portion)
*Beaune Premier Cru Clos Des Mouches*
*A lightly oaked Burgundy Chardonnay with notes of acacia, lime and hazelnuts*

-

Sauté of cèpes and prawns with spinach, sweet and sour vinaigrette
(page 168)

-

Supreme of pheasant with bacon and celery farce and a celery sauce
(page 186)
*Clos des Lambrays Grand Cru (8-10 years old, ideal in Magnums)*
*This is a mature Burgundy Pinot Noir with aromas of raspberries, chestnuts and truffles*

-

Poached quince with honey and ginger and a lightly spiced baba
(page 203)
*'Straw Wine' Chenin Blanc, Rustenberg Estate, South Africa*
*A fortified Chenin Blanc with notes of honey and baked apples*

# 'Autumn menu two'

Taster of celery soup with crispy celery leaves
(serve in a coffee cup)

-

Butternut squash custard flan with apple-walnut dressing and crispy onions
(page 165)
*Saint Clair Marlborough Riesling, New Zealand*
*This Riesling has a hint of sweetness and notes of lime and peach*

-

Loin of local lamb cooked in salt pastry, with wilted red and green chard,
tomato and chilli chutney and lamb jus
(page 189)
*La Rioja Alta Gran Reserva 890, Spain*
*This is a mature Tempranillo full of dates, summer fruit and coconut notes*

-

Selection of local cheeses served with pears steeped in red wine and ginger-rosemary
(taken from page 195)

-

Pistachio panna cotta with warm blackberries
(adapted from page 145)
*Vin Santo Del Chianti, Italy*
*A fortified Trebbiano/Malvasia wine with notes of dried grapes, honey, almonds*

## 'Winter menu one'

Taster of parsnip soup flavoured with wholegrain mustard
(served in a coffee cup)

~

Rabbit, Savoy cabbage and Pink Fir Apple potato terrine with sweet and sour style chicory
(page 225)
*Condrieu les Terrasses de L'Empire, Northern Rhone (1 year old)*
*A Viognier with notes of apricot, roses and honeysuckle*

~

Steamed cod fillet with stir-fried sprouting broccoli in sesame oil, tamarind dressing
(page 230, served as a half portion)

~

Roast loin of venison with salsify cooked in olive oil, and red wine sauce
(taken from page 235)
*Chateauneuf du Pape, Rhone (4-8 years old)*
*This is a Grenache/syrah full of blackberry, red and black pepper aromas*

~

Caramelised apple feuilleté with Madagascan vanilla cream and apple compote
(page 258)
*Vidal Icewine, Canada*
*This Icewine displays notes of frozen grapes, lemon and mango*

# 'Winter menu two'

Parsnip rosti with organic smoked bacon, thyme and horseradish crème fraîche
(page 224)

~

Salad of lobster with chicory, blood orange and crispy chorizo
(page 244)
*Taittinger Comtes de Champagne Rosé Brut*
*This champagne is well rounded and tastes full of red fruit*

~

Spiced and glazed belly pork with stir-fried Brussels sprouts
(page 246)
*Chassagne Montrachet Premier Cru, Burgundy*
*Cote de Beaune Burgundy Pinot Noir with aromas of raspberries, cherries and chestnuts*

*served with...*

Winter stew of curly kale, potatoes and truffles
(taken from page 242, served as a half portion/accompaniment)

~

Guanaja chocolate tart scented with fennel and chilli
(page 249)
*Quinta da Ervarmoira 10 year old Tawny Port*
*This is served as a light Tawny Port that has nutty, rich qualities*

# Glossary of terms

**Al dente**  This is an Italian term that translates 'to the tooth'. Normally refers to pasta and vegetables that are cooked until tender but still retain a 'bite'.

**Assiette**  A plated assortment of foods, normally along a theme.

**Baba**  A yeast-leavened cake which is soaked in a flavoured syrup.

**Bain Marie**  A saucepan/container of water that is used to melt or keep foods hot without burning them.

**Bavarois**  A sweet pudding made with eggs and cream and set with gelatine.

**Baveuse**  Normally refers to an omelette that is cooked underneath but slightly runny/soft on top.

**Blanching**  This originally meant to whiten by boiling, but now also refers to parboiling of vegetables for a minimal amount of time.

**Blind Bake**  This means to bake a pastry flan/tart case without the filling in order to cook the pastry first. Baking beans are used to prevent the pastry from collapsing or rising.

**Braising**  A method of cooking in the oven; the food is submerged in liquid and the pot covered.

**Brunoise**  Finely cubed (2-3mm) foods.

**Chinois**  A conical sieve which is used to strain sauces and jellies.

**Cocotte**  A small earthenware or porcelain dish normally used to cook eggs in.

**Compote**  Normally indicates stewed fruits; sometimes similarly cooked vegetables.

**Confit**  A French method of cooking that preserves food. Normally cooked in goose or duck fat, but also in olive oil.

**Dariole**  A small cylindrical mould used to make jellies, babas, mousses and panna cottas.

**Deglaze**  To swill out a pan with wine or stock in order to extract the flavour and sediment.

**Dock**  A term to describe pricking pastry with a fork to prevent it rising.

**Duxelle**  Very finely chopped mushrooms and onions/shallot that have been cooked until all the liquid has evaporated.

**Emulsified**  A mixture of two or more ingredients that does not separate on standing.

**En papillote**  The wrapping of a food in baking parchment or foil and then baking it.

**Ferment**  The conversion of starch and sugars into carbon dioxide bubbles.

**Feuilleté**  Baked puff pastry which can be filled or garnished with various savoury or sweet mixtures.

**Fricassee**  A light white stew thickened with cream, made with chicken, veal or vegetables.

**Gratinate**  To brown under a hot grill or in a hot oven

**Hull**  To remove the stalk and hard white part from a strawberry by using a knife to make a small circular and conical hole.

| | |
|---|---|
| **Infuse** | To soak foods in order to extract flavour. |
| **Julienne** | Vegetables, fruit or citrus peel cut into very fine matchsticks. |
| **Knead** | To work dough to make it smooth and soft by stretching the gluten content. |
| **Knock back** | To knock or punch the air out of a dough before baking. |
| **Marinade** | To soak meat, fish or vegetables in an acidulated liquid or oil with herbs and possibly spices; this flavours and helps to tenderise the food. |
| **Pane** | To coat food in milk then flour; or flour followed by beaten egg and then breadcrumbs. |
| **Panko** | A type of breadcrumb commonly used in Oriental cookery. |
| **Poaching** | To cook food in water that is just below boiling point. |
| **Preserving** | A food product that has been treated to keep it for longer. |
| **Prove** | To allow a dough to rise in volume. |
| **Puree** | Liquidised, finely mashed or sieved foods such as fruits and vegetables. |
| **Quenelle** | Finely minced or pureed fish, meat or vegetable shaped with spoons into dumpling or rugby ball shapes. |
| **Reduce** | To reduce the quantity of a liquid to the concentrate flavour or thicken it by boiling or simmering the liquid. |
| **Refresh** | To plunge food (normally vegetables) into iced water to stop the cooking process. |
| **Rest** | Allowing meat and sometimes fish time to stand before cutting it in order to prevent juices escaping. |
| **Sauté** | A method of frying in oil and butter to quickly and evenly colour foods. |
| **Silpat** | A special non-stick Teflon coated baking mat that aids in the baking of pastry and biscuits. Silpats are available at quality cookware shops. |
| **Skimming** | To skim the surface of a liquid to remove impurities such as fat. |
| **Steep** | The storing and preserving of fruit or vegetables. |
| **Stewing** | To cook small pieces of food slowly in the minimum amount of liquid. The liquid then forms the sauce. |
| **Sur-le-plat** | Small earthenware or porcelain dishes that are normally used to cook egg dishes or crème brûlée. |
| **Sweating** | To cook food in oil or butter over a low to medium heat without colouring. |
| **Tapenade** | A finely crushed black olive paste flavoured with garlic and herbs. |
| **Tempura** | A very light batter used to deep-fry courgette flowers and other delicate vegetables. |
| **Zest** | The outer skin of a citrus fruit. Zest is obtained by thinly peeling the fruit, taking care not to remove any of the white pith with the zest. |

# Acknowledgments

Writing and producing a cookery book is a collaboration between many people. Firstly, I would like to thank The Lord Kirkham CVO and Lady Kirkham for providing me with the opportunity to write the book and for their encouragement and enthusiasm along the way. Secondly, I am indebted to Keith Henson who took the first class photographs throughout. Keith gave up his time and used all his valuable photographic experience to great effect. He also assisted with food styling and provided many useful tips on producing a book.

In March of 1998 I competed in, and won, the Roux Scholarship Final. Colleagues talk of pivotal moments in their formative working years; this was undoubtedly mine. The Roux Scholarship provided me with unrivalled training opportunities as well as the support of Michel and Albert Roux. I am extremely grateful to the Roux Brothers for this. Albert Roux commented on that day; "We have given him the boots, now it's up to him to use them". The Roux Scholarship is a competition that I would encourage every young, passionate and ambitious chef to enter. For more information, consult the Scholarship website: www.rouxscholarship.co.uk.

The walled kitchen garden on Lord Kirkham's estate obviously gave me the inspiration to write this book. A kitchen garden does not look after itself and I have great admiration for the team of gardeners who see to every aspect of maintaining it to such a high standard. The team is led by Ian Fretwell who is assisted by Catherine Rainer (Glasshouse Foreman and Beekeeper), Robert Crossland, Rachel Middleton and Dave Long.

I must also thank Valerie Dyer, Derek Mould, Kerry Horne, John Leake, Andrew Heaton (Print Manager), Peter Thoday, Jerome McCulla, Otto Hinderer (Master Sommelier) and my parents, Peter and Carol Thompson, who have all assisted with proof reading, wine recommendations and design ideas. My fiancée, Natalie Phillips, has given me unrivalled support and encouragement, as well as proof reading during the 2 years that I have been working on this book, and for that I will always be grateful. Dave Hughes kindly supplied the game used throughout the book. Lastly and by no means least, many thanks to Denby who supplied me with a range of beautiful plates on which to present my food.

# Supplier information

However plentiful your kitchen garden, greenhouse or vegetable patch is, there will always be times when you need to outsource for ingredients. Shopping for food is very much a personal choice affected by your preferences and experiences of different food outlets. I have provided a list of the suppliers that I like to use. You will find that these are both local and national. As I mentioned on page 11, I try to take account of 'food miles' and wherever possible, coordinate my purchasing carefully to reduce excess journeys and transportation – every little helps.

<u>Vegetables and fruit:</u> hopefully your own garden.

Local markets, farmers' markets and farm shops.

'Box schemes' provide you with a box of seasonal fruit and vegetables which is delivered to your door and are run by several companies. A search on the internet should reveal the closet to you. The companies running box schemes include Abel & Cole, Riverford, Farmaround, Brown Cow Organics and Organic Delivery.

<u>Fish:</u>

Your local quality fish market.

*Doncaster Fish Market:* Martyns Famous Fish Stall (no11). 01302 761711. Open on Tuesday, Thursday, Friday and Saturday. Pre-orders welcome.

*Solstice:* Mail-order Company run by an award winning chef. www.solstice.co.uk

<u>Meat, game and poultry:</u>

Your local traditional butcher, farmers' markets and farm shop.

*Wilkinson's Butchers:* Doncaster Market and Bawtry. 01302 710496.

*Donald Russell:* Mail-order Company specialising in grass-fed cattle and lamb. www.donaldrussell.co.uk

*Yorkshire Game:* Locally caught and traceable game including partridge, pheasant, grouse and venison. www.yorkshiregame.co.uk

*Label Anglais:* These chickens spend at least 80 days scratching around and meat is consequently richer and stronger tasting than those insipid supermarket birds. www.labelanglais.co.uk

## Cheese and dairy:

*Neil's Cheese Board:* Doncaster Indoor market. 01427628166. www.neilscheeseboard.co.uk

*Neal's Yard Dairy:* A pioneer of British cheeses. You can order by mail order. www.nealsyarddairy.co.uk

## Herbs:

*Jekkas Herb Farm:* Mail-order Company for all your culinary and medicinal herbs both in seed form and plants. www.jekkasherbfarm.co.uk

*PSI Nursery:* located in Braithwell, South Yorkshire, this company can supply you with a range of exotic plants and herbs. www.psinursery.co.uk.

## Specialist produce:

*Solstice:* Purveyors of fine foods including fresh produce, condiments and dry foods. www.solstice.co.uk

*Wild harvest:* Mail-order Company specialising in wild mushrooms as well as seasonal vegetables and fruits, spices, rare-breed meat and poultry. www.wildharvestuk.com

*Slow Food:* This Society, founded in 1986 in Italy promotes food and wine culture and defends food and agricultural biodiversity all over the world. It has excellent links with local food producers and their retail outlets. www.slowfood.com

Farm visits and farm food purchases: Have a look at the *Soil Association* website where there are links to local farm visits and farmers' markets. www.soilassociation.org

## Wine suppliers:

When it comes to purchasing wine, particularly the wines recommended on pages 273 – 280, I suggest the following supplier:

*Otto Hinderer, Master Sommelier*
*The Cellar Masters Wine Company*
*Maycroft, 93 West Lane*
*Sharlston*
*Wakefield*
*WF4 1EP*
*01924 862229*
*01924 860331 (Fax)*

## Specialist cookery equipment:

www.nisbets.co.uk

www.ccs.net

# Ingredient index

I have listed below an index of the principal ingredients which are contained within The Essence.